Dhyan

Understanding Thai

Language
and
Grammar

BOOKS
www.dolphinbooks.org

Learning Thai Quickly and Easily

Publisher:

Dolphin Books

info@dolphinbooks.org

www.dolphinbooks.org

ISBN 978-952-6651-46-0

Acknowledgement

I would like to thank the following people for valuable guidance on Thai syntax and grammar, and assistance with editing and proofreading the text to reflect standard spoken Thai:

Ms. Duangmon Loprakhong, Thai Teacher, Duke Language School, Bangkok

Ms. Waree Singhanart, Thai Teacher, Bangkok

Mr. Watit Pumyoo, Chiang Mai University, Chiang Mai

I am also grateful to Mr. Walter Kassela for editing and proofreading the English text.

With the help of the above people, the clarity of the written Thai and English text has been significantly improved.

Special thanks to Duke Language School for kind co-operation.

Table of Contents

Introduction

In order to speak Thai fluently, you should know about 1500 to 2000 words commonly used by Thais everyday. You should also how the language works – how to use these words in a sentence. The common problem for foreigners who are studying Thai is how to learn new words and how to pronounce them. This book helps you on the way to reach your goal – to speak Thai fluently. It contains more than 1500 of the most common Thai words. They have been organized according to the relevant subject matter and grammatical function. There are many examples of sentences and tips on how to use these words.

Many of the commonly used Thai words in this this book have been borrowed from foreign languages such as Pali/Sanskrit, Chinese, Khmer, English, etc. Words have been grouped according to their meaning and usage. They are not in alphabetical order so you will learn Thai easier.

If you are a beginner, we would like to point out that in Thailand there are many different transliteration systems (sometimes also called romanization systems). That can be confusing but not much can be done about it. We recommend that you learn first one system well, such as the one used in this book. When you know all the sounds of the Thai language, it is easier for you to understand other systems. This is very important since you need to rely on transliterations when learning new words. To learn new words from the Thai script can be very challenging, at least in the beginning.

We have made your task easier by writing every word with simple and understandable phonetic transliteration symbols. Many of these symbols, particularly consonant symbols, are familiar to you already.

Some vowel symbols need to be written by new phonetic symbols since English vowels are not pronounced consistently. Our presentation contains all 20 Thai consonant sounds, 18 pure vowel sounds, and the five Thai tones.

It is quite important to gain an overall understanding of the Thai language. You don't need to know the Thai writing system in order to speak Thai fluently. It is very complex containing sophisticated tone rules and a vast number of consonants (42 altogether) representing only 20 different consonant sounds. This is due to the fact that many foreign words borrowed from languages such as Pali and Sanskrit use rare consonant symbols for the same common Thai sounds. Note, however, that these borrowed words, spelled with different consonant symbols (called rare consonants), do not add any more sounds to the Thai language. Only the spelling is different.

It makes sense in the beginning to concentrate on sounds. So, your priority should be in learning all the sounds of the Thai language well, use simple everyday words and know how the words are used in a sentence. Then, you will be able to interact with your Thai friends in their own language in a confident and relaxed way.

How to use this book?

This book has been designed to be used alone or as a supplement to any other Thai learning book. It contains twenty-three chapters. You may choose any chapter or section and study them separately according to your priorities. Once you get acquainted with this book, it is easy to find those sections which are of interest to you. In order to facilitate your studies, you may wish to use, alongside with this book, the following book which has been designed for beginners and intermediate language students.

Learning Thai with Original Thai Words
– Learning Thai Quickly and Easily
(ISBN 978-952-6651-43-9)

Chapter 1

Introduction to sounds and Thai transliteration

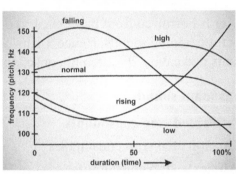

Tone Chart of "Jackson Gandour" (1976)

By knowing how new sounds are spoken both in theory and practice, you will become more confident in learning Thai. Then practise and adjust your speaking until you can make new sounds correctly.

This presentation includes all consonant and vowel sounds used in central Thai. However, there are consonant symbols in Thai script, and also some vowel sounds which can be written in several different ways.

In Thai, there are altogether 20 consonant sounds and 18 pure vowel sounds.

If in doubt, please review this section and also read the book *22 Secrets of Learning Thai – Complete Guide to Sounds, Tones and Thai Writing System*.

Many foreign words borrowed from Pali, Sanskrit or Khmer use rare consonants for common sounds. Hence, in the Thai alphabet list, 42 consonants make only 20 different consonant sounds.

1.1 **Thai consonant sounds**

    1.1.1 **Aspirated stop consonants**

    1.1.2 **Unaspirated stop consonants**

    1.1.3 **Affricate stop consonants**

    1.1.4 **Voiced stop consonants**

    1.1.5 **Fricative consonant sounds**

    1.1.6 **Sonorant consonant sounds**

1.2 **Thai vowel sounds**

1.3 **End sounds**

    1.3.1 **Open end sounds**

    1.3.2 **Closed end sounds**

    1.3.3 **Glottal stop**

1.4 **Consonant clusters**

    1.4.1 **Traditional Thai consonant clusters**

    1.4.2 **English consonant clusters used in Thai**

1.1 Thai consonant sounds

Basically, there are three types of consonant sounds in Thai, namely *stop consonant sounds, fricative consonant sounds* and *sonorant consonant sounds*. This distinction is very important in Thai in order to understand the Thai writing system and tones.

1.1.1 Aspirated stop consonants

Stop consonant sounds can be divided into four basic categories, namely *aspirated consonants, unaspirated consonants, affricate consonants* and *voiced consonants*.

Aspiration means that there is a puff of air coming out of your mouth when you produce the sound. Stop consonants are produced in such a way that air is first stopped by the lips or by the tongue and then released.

phɔɔ ฟ, thɔɔ ท, khɔɔ ค

- the letter **h** is used to denote the fact that the sound is aspirated with the puff of air

Thai words:

phaan	พาน	*tray*
phûng	ผึ้ง	*bee*
phɛɛng	แพง	*expensive*
tháhǎan	ทหาร	*soldier*
thǔng	ถุง	*bag*
thêep	เทพ	*God*
khwaai	ควาย	*water buffalo*
khài	ไข่	*egg*
khon	คน	*person*

Similar English sounds: **P**eter, **p**erson, **p**aper, **t**ime, **t**ake, **t**one, **k**iss, **k**ey, **k**eep

Rating: Good

- these sounds are not difficult for English speakers since similar consonant sounds in English are always aspirated at the beginning of a word or a syllable
- put your hand in front of the mouth, and feel that there is a puff of air coming when you say these words either in Thai or in English

1.1.2 Unaspirated stop consonants

When the sound is unaspirated, it means that there isn't any puff of air coming out of your mouth when you produce this sound. The sound is first stopped by the lips or by the tongue and then released in such a way, that there is no any puff of air coming out of your mouth when you make this consonant sound. The air is somehow stopped in the glottis. This is called in phonetic terms "glottal stop".

pɔɔ ป, **t**ɔɔ ต, **k**ɔɔ ก

Thai words:

plaa	ปลา	*fish*
pìt	ปิด	*to close*
pìip	ปีบ	*cork tree*
tàu	เต่า	*turtle*
tên	เต้น	*to dance*
tiin	ตีน	*foot* (not polite)
kài	ไก่	*chicken*
kɛ̀	แกะ	*to unwrap*
kɛ̀ɛ	แก่	*to be old*

Similar English sounds: s**p**eak, s**p**ell, s**p**y, s**t**op, s**t**ink, s**t**ate, s**k**in, s**k**ate, s**k**y

Rating: Not very good

- the tricky point is that in English we don't have unaspirated consonant sounds at the beginning of a word or a syllable
- we have therefore taken as examples similar consonant sounds in the middle of the word where the English aspiration is weak
- put your hand in front of the mouth, and make sure that there is no puff of air coming when you say these Thai words
- you may need some practice before getting the pronunciation of these words right without any puff of air. Do not hesitate to consult your Thai teacher

1.1.3 Affricate stop consonants

Affricate consonant sounds consist of two sounds at the beginning of the word, **tʃ** or **ts**. They can be either aspirated or unaspirated.

These affricate stop consonant sounds are produced in such a way that the air is first stopped by the tongue and then released.

tʃɔɔ ช and tsɔɔ จ

In Thai there are two affricate stop consonant sounds, **tʃ** as in the word **tʃɔɔp** ชอบ and **ts** as in the word **ts**ing จริง. The first sound in Thai is aspirated, and the second is unaspirated. English also has two affricate sounds, **tʃ** as in the word **c**hild and **dʒ** as in the word **j**ob. The first sound in English is aspirated, and the second is voiced.

English stop sounds at the beginning of a word are usually divided into aspirated and voiced. In Thai, the similar initial sounds are aspirated or unaspirated.

tʃɔɔ ช

Thai words:

tʃáang	ช้าง	*elephant*
tʃìng	ฉิ่ง	*cymbals*
tʃɛ̌ɛ	แฉ	*to reveal, to show*

Similar English sounds: **child, ch**oose, **ch**apter

Rating: Good

- you may use the English sound and there should not be any problem
- put your hand in front of the mouth, and feel that there is a puff of air coming when you say these words either in Thai or in English

tsɔɔ จ

The sound **tsɔɔ จ** is perhaps the most misunderstood Thai sound among non-native speakers. Therefore, we try to explain it here in detail.

This Thai sound **tsɔɔ จ** is transliterated in many ways, examples include: **j, ch, c, dsch**. The most correct way to transliterate this sound would be to use the international phonetic symbol **tɕ**. It is not known very well, however, and therefore seldom used. We have decided to use simply **ts**.

Thai words:

tsaan	จาน	*plate*
tsùm	จุ่ม	*to dip*
tsùu	จู่	*to rush*

Similar English sounds for **tsɔɔ จ**: **g**in, **j**oy, **ts**unami

Rating: Not very good

- the letter **j**, as in the English word **j**oy, is often given as an example. This is, however, not quite right, since the English consonant **j** is voiced, but the Thai sound **ts จ** is unvoiced
- note that if you pronounce the word **ts**unami as it is written and not like **s**unami, you are close
- make sure that you start with **t**-sound and then glide into **s**-sound. Put your hand in front of the mouth, and feel that there is not much air coming from your mouth when you say the above Thai words
- note also that English sounds, which are not aspirated at the beginning of the word are usually voiced. This Thai sound **tsɔɔ จ** is not voiced, not aspirated but unaspirated

- tsunami is a foreign word and is pronounced in several different ways by English speakers and therefore it is not a very good example

- the same type of foreign sound is the Russian word **ts**ar

- why is this sound difficult for English speakers? The reason is because there is no such sound at the beginning of English words. The same sound exists frequently at the end of the word in English. Good examples are: Le**t's**, ca**ts**, ha**ts**, bi**ts**, etc...

- note, however, if you pronounce this sound as in the English word **j**ob, you will be understood by Thais since there is no similar voiced sound in Thai for it to be confused with. In that case your pronunciation is not quite correct

1.1.4 Voiced stop consonants

Voiced sounds in Thai and in English are not aspirated. They are produced in such a way that vocal folds are vibrating. The sound is first stopped by the lips or by the tongue and then released.

bɔɔ บ, **d**ɔɔ ด

Thai words:

bai máai	ใบ ไม้	*leaf*
bin	บิน	*to fly*
bìip	บีบ	*to squeeze*
dèk	เด็ก	*child*
dù	ดุ	*to scold*
duu	ดู	*to look, to see*
din	ดิน	*land, earth*

Similar English sounds: **b**aby, **b**anana, **b**ig, **d**inner, **d**uck, **d**ance

Rating: Good

- here there is no problem at all. The English sounds are very similar to the Thai sounds

- note, however, that at the beginning of a word or a syllable the consonant sounds in English are either voiced or aspirated, but in Thai they can be aspirated, unaspirated and also voiced

1.1.5 Fricative consonant sounds

Fricative consonant sounds are produced in such a way that the air is not stopped but directed through a narrow channel. The turbulent airflow makes a friction. In Thai there are only two fricative sounds, namely **f** and **s**. Fricative consonant sounds in Thai are unvoiced.

In English there are three fricative sounds, **f**, **s** and **z**. In Thai the voiced counterpart **z** does not exist.

In order to be complete, we need to add one more fricative sound, the glottal fricative sound **h**, which is used similarly in Thai and in English.

fɔɔ ฟ, ซ s ɔɔ, **h**ɔɔ ฮ

Thai words:

fan	ฟัน	*teeth*
fǎa	ฝา	*lid, cover*
fǔung	ฝูง	*group, flock*
sôo	โซ่	*chain*
sǔua	เสือ	*tiger*
sǔun	ศูนย์	*zero*
nók **hûuk**	นกฮูก	*owl*
hìip	หีบ	*chest*
hɛ̂ɛng	แห้ง	*dry*

Similar English sounds: five, fax, form, seven, simple, same, he, have, host

Rating: Good

- if you use the English pronunciation for these three sounds, there should be no problems

1.1.6 Sonorant consonant sounds

The term sonorant sound means that the sound can be prolonged without any difficulty. The sound is not stopped by lips or by tongue. Sonorant sounds play a very important role as far as the Thai writing system is concerned. They are:

mɔɔ ม, nɔɔ น, lɔɔ ล, rɔɔ ร, ngɔɔ ง, yɔɔ ย and wɔɔ ว

Most sonorant sounds are pronounced in a similar way in Thai and in English.

If you use the English pronunciation for the following sonorant consonant sounds, there should be no problems.

There are, however, two sounds that we would like to explain in more detail, namely rɔɔ ร and ngɔɔ ง.

mɔɔ ม

Thai words:

máa	ม้า	*horse*
mău	เหมา	*to presume, to rent*
mâai	ม่าย	*widow*

Similar English sounds: **mother, make, main**

Rating: Good

nɔɔ น

nŭu	หนู	*mouse*
nâu	เน่า	*rotten*
năau	หนาว	*cold*

Similar English sounds: **nine, nice, not**

Rating: Good

lɔɔ ล

ling	ลิง	*monkey*
lăi	ไหล	*flow*
lăai	หลาย	*many*

Similar English sounds: line, lips, loose

Rating: Good

rɔɔ ร

Thai words:

ruua	เรือ	*boat*
rai	ไร	*something*
raai	ราย	*item*

Similar English sounds: red, read, ripe

Rating: Not very good

- many Thai speakers substitute this **r** ร-sound with the **l** ล-sound as in the English world like. So, it is quite common that Thai is spoken without the correct Thai **r** ร-sound
- when the correct **r** ร-sound is used by Thais, it is not exactly the same sound as the English **r**-sound
- Thai **r** is rolled more like the Spanish **r**
- some English speakers may produce this sound differently depending on origin of the country, education, etc...

ngɔɔ ง

Thai words:

nguu	งู	*snake*
ngong	งง	*to be confused*
ngóong	โง้ง	*to be bent*

English words: ki**ng**, si**ng**ing, fi**ng**er

Rating: Not very good

- this sound **ng** ง appears in several combinations in the English language
- however, it can prove quite difficult for English speaking learners to use this sound at the beginning of a word. This shows how strongly language skills are based on habits
- you may practise this sound by saying the first part of the word si**nging** silently and the second part loudly

yɔɔ ย

Thai words:

yák	ยักษ์	*giant*
yím	ยิ้ม	*smile*
yîiam	เยี่ยม	*excellent*

Similar English sounds: **y**ellow, **y**es, **y**ear

Rating: Good

wɔɔ ว

Thai words:

wɛ̆ɛn	แหวน	*ring*
wai	ไว	*fast*
wǎai	หวาย	*wicker palm*

Similar English sounds: **w**omen, **w**ife, **w**inter

Rating: Good

1.2 Thai vowel sounds

In Thai there are 9 short and 9 long pure vowel sounds. With these 18 vowel sounds you will be able to make all Thai vowel sounds including diphthongs and all other vowel combinations.

The main obstacle with the Thai vowel sounds for English speakers is to learn to separate short vowel sounds from their long counterparts. In Thai, vowels are produced clearly short or long.In English the pronunciation of vowels can vary depending on the person and the accent. Often in English the short vowels can be prolonged or long vowels shortened without loosing the meaning of the word. This can't be done with Thai vowels.

Note also that when we transliterate the vowel sounds, we write a short sound with one symbol and a long sound with two symbols. Some transliteration systems do not separate short and long vowels. Then there is no way to know how to pronounce those vowels. If you don't pronounce Thai vowels clearly, Thai people will have difficulty to understand you.

	Front	Central	Back
Closed	ิ อิ, ii อี	ึ อี, ืือ อือ	ุ อุ, uu อู
Half open	เ เอะ, ee เอ	่ เออะ, əə เออ	่ โอะ, oo โอ
Open	็ แอะ, ɛɛ แอ	่ อะ, aa อา	่ เอาะ, ɔɔ ออ

ิ อิ and ii อี

Learn to separate the short ิ อิ-sound from its long counterpart ii อี.

Thai words:

bì	ปิ̀	*to break off*
bìip	ปีบ	*to squeeze, to press*
pìt	ปิด	*to close*
pìip	ปีบ	*cork tree*
bin	บิน	*to fly*
biin	บีน	(only a sound, no meaning)

Similar English sounds for short ì อิ: happy, think, sit

Similar English sounds for long ii อี: see, meat, teach

Rating: Good

- if you use the English pronunciation for the short ì อิ and long ii อี -sounds, there should be no problems
- just make sure that the short sound is short and the long sound clearly long
- note also that some English speakers, particularly Americans, tend to make this sound similar to an e-sound as in the English word pet

ч อึ and чч อือ

Learn to separate the short ч อึ-sound from its long counterpart чч อือ.

It is often said that there is no comparable sound in English for these two sounds. This is not quite true, since some English speakers, even in England and the USA, seem to use a similar sound with words like could, should, good, cute, few and rude. Others pronounce the same sound differently.

Thai words:

phùng	ผึ่ง	to dry, to expose
phùun	ผืน	prickly
bûng	บึ้ง	to be serious
pûun	ปื้น	eruption on the skin
phûng	ผึ้ง	bee
phǔun	ผืน	sheet

Similar English sounds for short ч อึ: should, good, would

Similar English sounds for long чч อือ: cute, few, rude

Rating: Not good

- listen to the audio and try to adjust your sound to conform with the Thai sound

- if you are facing difficulties, we would advise you to find a good native Thai teacher to get this sound right since you can't directly use the English sounds

- remember to make a short sound short and a long vowel sound clearly long

ù อุ and **uu** อู

Note that the long English **uu** อู-sound is sometimes pronounced differently by different English speakers. Some may use a version similar to the Thai sound, **ʉʉ** อือ. This happens often with words like new, dew, g**oo**d, t**wo**.

Do not mix up these two sounds **ù** อุ and **ʉ** อึ or **uu** อู and **ʉʉ** อือ. In Thai, they are clearly different sounds. In English, the distinction is not so clear.

Thai words:

fùn	ฝุ่น	*dust*
fǔung	ฝูง	*group*
pù	ปุ	*to patch*
pùu	ปู่	*grandfather*
bun	บุญ	*merit*
phuun	พูน	*to pile up*

Similar English sounds for short **ù** อุ: l**oo**k, p**u**t, f**oo**t

Similar English sounds for long **uu** อู: c**oo**l, s**oo**n, d**o**

Rating: Quite good, but pay attention

- do not mix up the short **ù** อุ with the short **ʉ** อึ
- do not mix up the long **uu** อู with the long **ʉʉ** อือ

- they are made in a similar way. **ù** อุ and **uu** อู are made with rounded lips and **u** อึ and **uu** อือ are made with unrounded lips

è เอะ and **ee** เอ

The short **è** เอะ and the long **ee** เอ-sounds do not exist in their pure form in Standard English.

Thai words:

thét	เท็จ	*false, incorrect*
thêet	เทศ	*foreign*
pen	เป็น	*to be*
pheen	เพล	*lunch time (monk)*
pèt	เป็ด	*duck*
thêep	เทพ	*god, divine being*

Similar English sounds for short **è** เอะ: pet, said, bread

Rating: Quite good, but pay attention

Similar English words for long **ee** เอ: pale, paint, sail

Rating: Not very good

- some English speakers pronounce the short **è** เอะ sound in English close to the Thai sound **è** แอะ while others may pronounce it differently
- note that in Thai vowel sounds can't be changed in any way. They need to be pronounced clearly
- the long **ee** เอ sound doesn't exist in its pure form in Standard English
- if you pronounce the **ee** เอ sound as in the English word pale like peeil without the i-sound, you are close to this Thai sound
- listen to the audio and ask your native Thai teacher to correct your pronunciation in order to learn to get these two sounds exactly right

ə̀ เออะ and əə เออ

Learn to separate this short ə̀ เออะ-sound from its long counterpart əə เออ.

These two sounds appear in English often with the consonant **r**. In order to get the Thai sound right you should not pronounce the r-sound.

Thai words:

də̂n	เดิ้น	*smart* (slang)
dəən	เดิน	*to walk*
tə̀	เตอะ	(only a sound, no meaning)
təəm	เติม	*to fill, to add*
bə̀ng	เบิ่ง	*to look* (Isaan dialect)
pə̀ət	เปิด	*to open*

Similar English sounds for short ə̀ เออะ: **a**bout, teach**er**, Anglia

Similar English sounds for long əə เออ: h**er**, b**ir**d, b**urn**

Rating: Quite good, but pay attention

- if you speak American English, please be aware that you should pronounce short ə̀ เออะ and long əə เออ-sounds without the **r**-sound. If in doubt, ask your native teacher to help you get these sounds exactly right

ò โอะ and **oo** โอ

Be aware that in Thai, long and short vowels are pronounced the same, only the duration is different. These two sounds in English are usually turned into a vowel combination such as **ou** or **ə u**.

Please make sure that you are able to understand and produce these sounds correctly. You need to learn to make these sounds, short and long, without the **u**-sound.

Thai words:

son	ซน	*to be naughty*
soon	โซน	*zone, area*
sòt	สด	*fresh*
sòot	โสด	*single, unmarried*
tòt	ตด	*to fart*
dòot	โดด	*to jump*

Similar English sounds for short **ò** โอะ: f**o**lk, r**o**ll, b**o**lt

Similar English sounds for long **oo** โอ: g**o**, hell**o**, l**aw**

Rating: Not very good

- the short **ò** โอะ and the long **oo** โอ sounds do not exist in their pure form in Standard English
- for the short **ò** โอะ sound you need to learn to say the English word f**o**lk, without the **ù** อุ-sound
- for the long **oo** โอ you must learn to say the English word *go* without the **ù** อุ-sound as g**oo**
- make this long **oo** โอ-sound longer than the short **ò** โอะ. It is close to the long **ɔɔ** ออ-sound as in the English word **law**

ɛ̀ แอะ and ɛɛ แอ

Learn to separate the short **ɛ̀** แอะ-sound from its long counterpart **ɛɛ** แอ.

Thai words:

tʃɛ̀	แฉะ	*wet*
tʃɛ̌ɛ	แฉ	*to reveal, to show*
tsɛ̀	แจะ	*sound of chewing*
tsɛ̀ɛk	แจก	*to hand out*
kɛ̀	แกะ	*to unwrap*
kɛ̀ɛ	แก่	*to be old*

Similar English sounds for short **è** แอะ: cat, hang, **at**

Similar English sounds for long **ɛɛ** แอ: sad, bad, mad

Rating: Quite good, but pay attention

- if you use the English sound as in the word cat for the short **è** แอะ -sound, you are quite close

- if you use the English sound as in the word bad for the long **ɛɛ** แอ, you are quite close

- Note, however, that some English speakers tend to pronounce the long **ɛɛ** แอ as in the English word bad shorter than it is pronounced in Thai. Make sure that you always pronounce long vowel sounds long in Thai.

à อะ and **aa** อา

Note that in Thai, it is very important to maintain the correct length of a vowel. When the vowel length changes, the meaning of the word changes as well. In English the length of the vowel can be changed without loosing the meaning.

Thai words:

khâ	ค่ะ	ending particle
khâa	ค่า	*price*
kàt	กัด	*to bite*
kàat	กาด	*market* (Northern dialect)
khát	คัด	*to select, to copy*
khàat	ขาด	*to be missing*

Similar English sounds for short **à** อะ: **bu**t, run, fl**oo**d

Rating: Good

Similar English sounds for long **aa** อา: father, vast, passport

Rating: Quite good, but pay attention

- for the short Thai **à** อะ sound the English sound may be used without any difficulty as in the word r**u**n

- however, some English speakers, particularly Americans, tend to pronounce the long **aa** อา-sound similar to the sound in the English word s**a**d, written phonetically as sɛɛd. They tend to say pɛɛsport instead of p**aa**sport. You need to be careful not to change the quality of the sound when you produce these short and long vowels in Thai

- listen to the audio and then check with your native Thai teacher so that you can pronounce these two sounds clearly and exactly right

ɔ̀ เอาะ and ɔɔ ออ

Learn to distinguish the short **ɔ̀ เอาะ**-sound from its long counterpart **ɔɔ ออ**. Note that in Thai the difference between long and short vowel is only the length of the sound.

In English, however, changing the length of the vowel sound often makes a qualitatively different sound as it is the case with these two sounds.

You also need to learn to distinguish **ɔ̀ เอาะ** and **ɔɔ ออ** from **ò โอะ** and **oo โอ**. Even though these sounds are quite close, you need to learn to hear, understand and reproduce the difference.

Thai words:

hɔ̂ng	ห้อง	*room*
hɔ̌ɔm	หอม	*to smell good*
hɔ̂ng-gong	ฮ่องกง	*Hong Kong*
hɔ̀ɔ	ห่อ	*package*
tɔ̂ng	ต้อง	*must*
thɔ́ɔng	ท้อง	*stomach*

Similar English sounds for short **ɔ̀ เอาะ**: n**o**t, g**o**t, s**o**ft

Rating: Not very good

Similar English sounds for long ออ ออ: **all**, **c**au**ght**, **law**

Rating: Quite good

- standard English does not have the short อ เอาะ-sound in its pure form

- one way to explain the short อ เอาะ-sound is to use the long ออ ออ-sound as in the word **law** but make it short. You may need help from a native teacher to get this sound right

- if you make the long ออ ออ-sound as in the English word **law**, you will be quite close. In Thai, this vowel is perhaps pronounced more open than the similar vowel sound in English. More open means that you open your mouth a bit more

- do not mix up these two sounds, short อ เอาะ and short อ โอะ

- do not mix up these two sounds, long ออ ออ and long **oo** โอ

- they are made in a similar way

1.3 End sounds

End sound are very important in Thai since they have an effect on tones. End sounds are divided into two main groups, namely open end sounds and closed end sounds.

1.3.1 Open end sounds

Open end sounds, also called "live syllables", are formed when a word is ending with a so called *sonorant consonant sound* or *with a long vowel* or *with a long* and *short vowel combination*. One special feature of an open ending sound is that the sound can be continued without stopping it. All sonorant sounds are voiced, meaning that the vocal folds are vibrating. Hence, vowels are usually classified as sonorant sounds. Sonorant sounds are produced with a continuing resonant sound.

When reviewing end sounds, we have a chance to introduce also all the special vowels, diphthongs and vowel combinations in Thai. Open end sounds are produced in Thai in the similar way as in English. However, there are many more diphthongs or vowel combinations in Thai than in English.

All the sonorant consonants in Thai constitute an *open ending* when at the end of the word or syllable. Also all long vowels or vowel combinations constitute an open end sound.

a) **Sonorant consonants: n** น**, r** ร **(n) , l** ล **(n) m** ม**, ng** ง

b) **Any long pure vowel -sound in Thai constitute an** *open ending.* There are nine pure long vowel sounds in Thai: **aa** อา**, ii** อี**, uu** อู **, ee** เอ**, εε** แอ**, oo** โอ**, ɔɔ** ออ **, əə** เออ**, นน** อือ

c) **Special vowels**

Any special vowel constitutes an *open end sound.* They are: **am** อำ**, au** เอา**, ai** ใอ, ไอ

d) **Short vowel combinations**

Any short vowel combination constitutes an *open end sound.* In Thai, there are five short vowel combinations: **iu** อิว**, ui** อุย**, eu** เอ็ว**, ai** อัย

e) **Long diphthongs**

These three are long diphthongs in Thai: **iia** เอีย**, นนa** เอือ**, uua** อัว

f) **Long vowel combination**

Any long vowel combination constitutes an *open end sound.*

They are: **eeu** เอว**, əəi** เอย**, ooi** โอย**, εεu** แอว**, aai** อาย**, aau** อาว**, ɔɔi** ออย**, iiau** เอียว**, นนai** เอือย**, uuai** อวย

1.3.2 Closed end sounds

a) **Consonant end sounds**

There are only three closed consonant end sounds in Thai (**p, t, k**)

- บ (**b**), ป (**p**), พ ภ (**ph**), ฟ (**f**) = **p**
- ต ฏ (**t**), ถ ท ธ ฐ ฑ (**th**), ด ฎ (**d**), ซ ศ ษ ส (**s**), จ (**ts**), ช (**tʃ**) = **t**

● ก (**k**), ค ฆ, ข (**kh**) = **k**

Here we have 25 Thai consonant symbols which constitute only
three end sounds, **p**, **t** and **k**. At the beginning of the word, these
25 consonants are pronounced as **b, p, ph, f, d, t, th, s, ʧ, ts, k, kh**;
that is altogether only 12 sounds. Now, all these initial consonants
are somehow connected to the Thai tonal system. There are five
tones; hence, these 25 consonants produce a vast number of sounds
(different pronunciation with different tones) but only three end
sounds, **p**, **t** and **k**.

So, if the end sound is *dead,* you will see only these three stop
consonant sounds **p**, **t** and **k** in the transliteration. They are all
written differently in the Thai script (by 25 different consonant
symbols). You do not need to learn this since we are relying mainly
on transliterations in this book. However, we thought it would be
good for you to know this since it is a very basic feature of the
Thai writing system and sounds.

Examples: ʧɔ̌ɔ**p** ชอบ *to like,* tà**t** ตัด *to cut,* mâa**k** มาก *much*

b) **Short vowels**

All *short vowels* at the end of the word or syllable constitute a
closed ending. There are nine short vowels in Thai: ì อิ, ʉ̀ อึ, ù อุ,
è เอะ, ɔ̀ เออะ, ò โอะ, ɛ̀ แอะ, à อะ, ɔ̀ เอาะ

They are suddenly stopped in the glottis and are kind of "buried"
in the mouth in the similar way as the *stop consonants* **p**, **t** and **k**.

Examples: tó โต๊ะ *table,* phrɔ́ เพราะ *because,* thɔ̀ เถอะ *particle for
emphasis*

c) **Short diphthongs**

ìa เอียะ, **ʉ̀a** เอือะ, **ùa** อัวะ

There are only three short diphthongs in Thai script. Short diphthongs are not used very much in Thai. So, we give here only one
example, y**úa** ยัวะ *hot-tempered.*

1.3.3 Glottal stop

This term is mainly used to describe Thai closed end sounds. The glottal stop is a consonant or a vowel sound produced while the air flow is stopped in the vocal tract in the throat.

When the consonant stop sounds like **t**, **p** and **k** are made with the glottal stop, the sound is unaspirated without any puff of air. The sound is not released but kind of buried in the mouth.

This is a very important sound to understand when making the unaspirated stop sounds in Thai. All short vowel sounds at the end of the word or syllable are made with a glottal stop in Thai.

Several British or American dialects use a glottal stop with end sounds like ca**t**, si**p** or sa**ck**. Cockney English dialect is a very good example of when English sounds are made with a glottal stop. See more about how to make a glottal stop on the web page:

http://www.youtube.com/watch?v=edxwQK1zBxw&list

If you understand how to make a glottal stop sound, it will help immensely with your Thai studies. Note however that you cannot ask your Thai friends or even your Thai teachers about the glottal stop unless they are trained in phonetics. They know how to make the sound, but they may not know what the glottal stop is.

1.4 Consonant clusters

A consonant cluster is formed by two consonant sounds. In the English language, there are many more consonant clusters than in Thai. Some common English clusters are: **bl**ue, **pr**actice, **fr**ee, **st**udent, **sp**ine, etc. So, English speakers are used to make these sounds even though consonant clusters can be made from different consonants in Thai. Just learn Thai consonant clusters as they come. There is no point to try to memorize all ways to make consonant clusters in Thai.

In English and Thai, consonant clusters are used in a similar way. For example, the cluster **pr** in the Thai word **pràp** ปรับ and in the English word **pr**actise sound the same.

1.4.1 Traditional Thai consonant clusters

Consonant clusters in Thai are made from the following consonant combinations:

kw กว, **kr** กร, **kl** กล, **khw** ขว-คว, **khr** ขร-คร, **khl** ขล-คล, **tr** ตร, **pr** ปร, **pl** ปล, **phr** พร, **phl** ผล-พล

Note that many Thais do not pronounce consonant clusters clearly, and some clusters are commonly omitted completely in casual speech. So, you just have to get used to it. For example the cluster **pl**aa ปลา *fish* is sometimes spoken as **paa**.

1.4.2 English consonant clusters used in Thai

There are a few more clusters borrowed from English. These clusters do not appear in original Thai words. They appear only in English loan words.

Examples:

frii	ฟรี	*to be free*
flét	แฟลต	*flat, apartment*
brèek	เบรก	*to brake*
bluu	บลูส์	*blues*
sà**k**ii*	สกี	*ski*

* This cluster is special since Thais like to add **a**-vowel between the cluster. It is easier to pronounce that way.

◊

Chapter 2

Original Thai words compared to foreign origin words

Original Thai words and words borrowed from Chinese are normally *one-syllable* words while other foreign words may have two or more syllables. Therefore, original Thai words are hard to distinguish from Chinese words since they are also written with the most common consonants as the original Thai words are written.

It is quite easy to point out those words, which have been borrowed from Khmer, English or Pali and Sanskrit into Thai. They are often spelled differently in the Thai script using so called rare consonants. They also often have more than one syllable.

We just thought that it would be good to know this; it will make it easier for you to understand the logic behind the Thai language and the writing system.

2.1   Common original Thai words

2.2   Common Chinese words

2.3   Common Khmer words

2.4   Common Pali/Sanskrit words

2.5   Common English words

2.1 Common original Thai words

Original Thai words are used as glue to join together words borrowed from other languages. It is not really possible to make meaningful sentences without a good knowledge of original Thai words since they perform important grammatical functions.

Examples:

lɛ́	และ	*and*
yùu	อยู่	*to stay, to live*
tsà	จะ	*will*
khɤɤi	เคย	*used to*
phɯ̂ng	เพิ่ง	*just*
mii	มี	*to have*
pai	ไป	*to go*
maa	มา	*to come*
pen	เป็น	*to be*
tham	ทำ	*to do*
mâi	ไม่	*no*
wâa	ว่า	*to say, that*
níi	นี้	*this*
kàp	กับ	*with*
tɛ̀ɛ	แต่	*but*
thîi	ที่	*that, which, to, at...*
khon	คน	*person*
rau	เรา	*we*
miia	เมีย	*wife* (colloquial)
phǔua	ผัว	*husband* (colloquial)

Original Thai words are normally one-syllable words.

2.2 Common Chinese words

The Chinese words have been borrowed from different Chinese dialects into Thai hundreds of years ago. They have been assimilated very well into Thai. Therefore, it is not always easy to point out which words are borrowed from Chinese since they are normally written with the most common consonants in the Thai script.

Examples:

lέεu	แล้ว	*already*
ngən	เงิน	*money*
chaa	ชา	*tea*
jee	เจ	*vegetarian*
kài	ไก่	*chicken*
suuai*	ซวย	*bad luck*
kεεng	แกง	*soup*
tʃɛ̌ɛ	แฉ	*to reveal, to show*
tó	โต๊ะ	*table*
phâi	ไพ่	*card, card game*
máa	ม้า	*horse*
tâu-hûu	เต้า หู้	*tofu*
kâu-îi	เก้าอี้	*chair*

* The Chinese word **suuai** ซวย means in Thai *bad luck*. However, the Thai word **sǔuai** สวย with a different tone means *beautiful*.

The Chinese words are normally one-syllable words.

2.3 Common Khmer words

Many Khmer origin words have been borrowed into Thai. They are often two-syllable words. One special feature is that often the vowel sound in Khmer script is omitted in writing but clearly pronounced in speaking. Hence, the Thai language follows this rule when a word is borrowed from Khmer. For example, the Khmer origin word **thà-nǒn**

ถนน *road* has two vowel sounds, but the word is written only with
three consonants. The vowel sounds are not written but pronounced.

Examples:

sà-àat	สะอาด	*to be clean*
săm-ràp	สำหรับ	*for*
trùu-at	ตรวจ	*to check, to inspect*
phà-sŏm	ผสม	*to mix*
thà-nŏn	ถนน	*road, street*
kam-lang	กำลัง	*power, present time tense marker*
sòk-kà-pròk*	สกปรก	*dirty*

* Note that **sòk-kà-pròk** สกปรก *dirty* has three syllables and is written
  with four consonants (**s, k, p, k**) in the Thai script. Yet, this word
  is pronounced with three vowel sounds (**o, a, o**). Very interesting!
  There is not any original Thai word that is written in this manner.

Many Khmer origin words are multi-syllables.

2.4 Common Pali/Sanskrit words

Many Indic origin words (Pali/Sanskrit) are two-syllable words. One
particular feature is that a large part of the vocabulary borrowed from
Pali/Sanskrit is written with rare Thai consonants which are not normally used with the original Thai words. Therefore, it is quite easy to
identify these words in the vocabulary.

Examples:

phaasăa	ภาษา	*language*
àksɔ̆ɔn	อักษร	*alphabetic letter*
sŏmbuun	สมบูรณ์	*to be perfect*
sàwăn*	สวรรค์	*heaven*
pràthêet	ประเทศ	*country*
phísèet*	พิเศษ	*to be special*
bɔɔrísàt	บริษัท	*company*

* Note that in these two words, we have three **s**-consonants. ส, ศ and ษ. Original Thai words are normally written with only one **s**-sound, ส.

Many Pali/Sanskrit words are written with the rare Thai consonant symbols.

2.5 Common English words

Words borrowed from English are often technical and modern vocabulary. They have been modified to suite a Thai pronunciation. Therefore, it is sometimes hard to get the meaning when Thais use words borrowed from English. The sound can be quite different. For example the consonant **s** is always pronounced as **t** at the end of the word and **s** at the beginning of the word. Hence **sɔɔwìs** (service) is pronounced as **sɔɔwìt**.

Examples:

tʃɔ́ɔppîng	ชอปปิ้ง	*shopping*
sentɔ̂ɔ	เซ็นเตอร์	*centre*
khɔɔmphíutɔ̂ɔ	คอมพิวเตอร์	*computer*
ápdèet	อัปเดต	*update*
wépsái	เว็บไซต์	*website*
sɔɔwìt	เซอร์วิส	*service*
hai-thèk	ไฮเทค	*high-tech*
inthɔɔnèt	อินเทอร์เน็ต	*internet*

One particular feature of English words is that the Thai language wants to keep the original English spelling. Therefore, the consonant **r** is written at the end of the word **sentɔ̂ɔ** เซ็นเตอร์ *centre* but not pronounced. When you see that small symbol on the top of the consonant, it means that this consonant is not pronounced. The same is true with Pali/Sanskrit words. Hence, whenever you see that small symbol called *karan* (ร์) on top of any consonant, you can assume that the word is borrowed either from English or Pali/Sanskrit.

◊

Chapter 3

**Personal pronouns, family members
and body parts**

3.1. Personal pronouns

phŏm	ผม	*I/male speaker*
tʃán	ฉัน	*I/female speaker*
dìtʃán	ดิฉัน	*I/female speaker* (formal)
khun	คุณ	*you* (singular)
phûuak-khun	พวก คุณ	*you* (plural)
kháu	เขา	*he, she*
thəə	เธอ	*she*
rau, phûuak-rau	เรา, พวก เรา	*we*
phûuak-kháu	พวก เขา	*they*
man	มัน	*it*

3.2 Family members and relatives

phɔ̂ɔ	พ่อ	*father*
mɛ̂ɛ	แม่	*mother*
phɔ̂ɔ-mɛ̂ɛ	พ่อ แม่	*parents*
phanráyaa	ภรรยา	*wife* (polite/Indic origin)
miia	เมีย	*wife* (colloquial/Thai origin)
sǎamii	สามี	*husband* (polite/Indic origin)
phǔua	ผัว	*husband* (colloquial/Thai origin)
lûuk-sǎau	ลูก สาว	*daughter*
lûuk-tʃaai	ลูก ชาย	*son*
nɔ́ɔng-tʃaai	น้อง ชาย	*younger brother*
nɔ́ɔng-sǎau	น้อง สาว	*younger sister*
phîi-tʃaai	พี่ ชาย	*older brother*
phîi-sǎau	พี่ สาว	*older sister*
lǎan	หลาน	*grandchild*
lǎan-tʃaai	หลาน ชาย	*grandson*

lǎan-sǎau	หลาน สาว	*granddaughter*
taa	ตา	*grandfather* (mother's father)
yaai	ยาย	*grandmother* (mother's mother)
pùu	ปู่	*grandfather* (father's father)
yâa	ย่า	*grandmother* (father's mother)
lûuk-líiang	ลูก เลี้ยง	*stepchild*
phɔ̂ɔ-líiang	พ่อ เลี้ยง	*stepfather*
mɛ̂ɛ-líiang	แม่ เลี้ยง	*stepmother*

3.3 Body parts

râang-kaai	ร่าง กาย	*body*
klâam-nɯ́ɯa	กล้าม เนื้อ	*muscle, muscles*
kràdùuk	กระดูก	*bone, bones*
phǐu	ผิว	*skin*
lɯ̂ɯat	เลือด	*blood*
hǔua	หัว	*head*
hǔu	หู	*ear, ears*
taa	ตา	*eye, eyes*
pàak	ปาก	*mouth*
rim-fǐi-pàak	ริม ฝี ปาก	*lip, lips*
lín	ลิ้น	*tongue*
thɔ́ɔng	ท้อง	*stomach*
khɔɔ	คอ	*neck, throat*
lǎng	หลัง	*back*
nâa-òk	หน้า อก	*chest*
mɯɯ	มือ	*hand, hands*
tháu	เท้า	*foot, feet*
níu	นิ้ว	*finger, toe*

níu-mɰɰ	นิ้ว มือ	*finger, fingers*
níu-tháu	นิ้ว เท้า	*toe, toes*
khɛ̌ɛn	แขน	*arm, arms, limb, limbs*
khǎa	ขา	*leg, legs*
hǔua-khàu	หัว เข่า	*knee, knees*
khɔ̂ɔ-sɔ̀ɔk	ข้อ ศอก	*elbow, elbows*
khɔ̂ɔ-mɰɰ	ข้อ มือ	*wrist, wrists*
khɔ̂ɔ-tháu	ข้อ เท้า	*ankle, ankles*

Chapter 4

Days, weeks, months and seasons

4.1 Days of the week

wan วัน *day* is normally placed before the names of the weekdays. All these words have been borrowed from Pali/Sanskrit.

wan-aathít	วัน อาทิตย์	*Sunday*
wan-tsan	วัน จันทร์	*Monday*
wan-angkhaan	วัน อังคาร	*Tuesday*
wan-phút	วัน พุธ	*Wednesday*
wan-phárúhàt	วัน พฤหัส	*Thursday*
wan-sùk	วัน ศุกร์	*Friday*
wan-său	วัน เสาร์	*Saturday*

4.2 Months

When the name of a month is ending with **khom,** that month has 31 days. When the name is ending with **yon,** that month has 30 days. **phan** is only used for February. The names of days and months are borrowed from Indic origin languages such as Pali/Sanskrit.

mókkàraa-khom	มกรา คม	*January*
kumphaa-phan	กุมภา พันธ์	*February*
miinaa-khom	มีนา คม	*March*
meesăa-yon	เมษา ยน	*April*
phrútsàphaa-khom	พฤษภา คม	*May*
míthùnaa-yon	มิถุนา ยน	*June*
kàrákàdaa-khom	กรกฎา คม	*July*
sĭnghăa-khom	สิงหา คม	*August*
kanyaa-yon	กันยา ยน	*September*
tùlaa-khom	ตุลา คม	*October*
phrútsàtsìkaa-yon	พฤศจิกา ยน	*November*
thanwaa-khom	ธันวา คม	*December*

We may also place the word **dʉʉan** เดือน month before the name of the month. So, **thanwaa-khom** ธันวา คม becomes **dʉʉan-thanwaa-khom** เดือน ธันวา คม *December.* Sometimes, Thais drop the second part and say **dʉʉan-thanwaa** เดือน ธันวา December.

If you don't remember the name of the month, you may also say **dʉʉan thîi sìp** เดือน ที่ สิบ *October* (tenth month of the year). Thais will understand you.

4.3 Seasons

rʉ́duu ฤดู *season* and **nâa** หน้า *season* are generally interchangeable.

nâa-rɔ́ɔn	หน้า ร้อน	*hot season, summer*
rʉ́duu-rɔ́ɔn	ฤดู ร้อน	*hot season, summer*
nâa-fǒn	หน้า ฝน	*rainy season*
rʉ́duu-fǒn	ฤดู ฝน	*rainy season*
nâa-nǎau	หน้า หนาว	*cold season, winter*
rʉ́duu-nǎau	ฤดู หนาว	*cold season, winter*
nâa-lέεng	หน้า แล้ง	*dry season*
rʉ́duu-lέεng	ฤดู แล้ง	*dry season*
rʉ́duu-bai-máai-rûuang*	ฤดู ใบ ไม้ ร่วง	*autumn, fall*
rʉ́duu-bai-máai-phlì*	ฤดู ใบ ไม้ ผลิ	*spring*

* These are Western type of seasons and are not normally used in Thailand.

◊

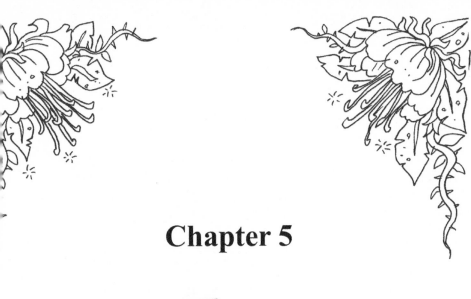

Chapter 5

Thai numbers

5.1   **Cardinal numbers**

5.2   **Ordinal numbers**

5.1 Cardinal numbers

Numbers are borrowed from Southern Chinese dialects and modified to suite the Thai pronunciation.

0	sǔun	ศูนย์
1	nùng	หนึ่ง
2	sɔ̌ɔng	สอง
3	sǎam	สาม
4	sìi	สี่
5	hâa	ห้า
6	hòk	หก
7	tsèt	เจ็ด
8	pὲὲt	แปด
9	kâau	เก้า
10	sìp	สิบ
11	sìp èt	สิบ เอ็ด
12	sìp sɔ̌ɔng	สิบ สอง
13	sìp sǎam	สิบ สาม
14	sìp sìi	สิบ สี่
15	sìp hâa	สิบ ห้า
16	sìp hòk	สิบ หก
17	sìp tsèt	สิบ เจ็ด
18	sìp pὲὲt	สิบ แปด
19	sìp kâau	สิบ เก้า
20	yîi sìp	ยี่ สิบ
21	yîi sìp èt	ยี่ สิบ เอ็ด
22	yîi sìp sɔ̌ɔng	ยี่ สิบ สอง
23	yîi sìp sǎam	ยี่ สิบ สาม

30	săam sìp	สาม สิบ
40	sìi sìp	สี่ สิบ
50	hâa sìp	ห้า สิบ
60	hòk sìp	หก สิบ
70	tsèt sìp	เจ็ด สิบ
80	pɛ̀ɛt sìp	แปด สิบ
90	kâau sìp	เก้า สิบ
99	kâau sìp kâau	เก้า สิบ เก้า
100	nùng rɔ́ɔi	หนึ่ง ร้อย
200	sɔ̌ɔng rɔ́ɔi	สอง ร้อย
300	săam rɔ́ɔi	สาม ร้อย
900	kâau rɔ́ɔi	เก้า ร้อย
1,000	nùng phan	หนึ่ง พัน
2,000	sɔ̌ɔng phan	สอง พัน
3,000	săam phan	สาม พัน
9,000	kâau phan	เก้า พัน
10,000*	nùng mɯ̀ɯn	หนึ่ง หมื่น
20,000	sɔ̌ɔng mɯ̀ɯn	สอง หมื่น
30,000	săam mɯ̀ɯn	สาม หมื่น
90,000	kâau mɯ̀ɯn	เก้า หมื่น
100,000	nùng sɛ̌ɛn	หนึ่ง แสน (1 hundred thousand)
1,000,000	nùng láan	หนึ่ง ล้าน (1 million)
10,000,000	sìp láan	สิบ ล้าน (10 million)
100,000,000	nùng rɔ́ɔi láan	หนึ่ง ร้อย ล้าน (100 million)
1,000,000,000	nùng phan láan	หนึ่ง พัน ล้าน (1 billion)

* Note that in Thai 10,000 is not **sìp phan** สิบ พัน *ten thousand*. It is written and spoken as **nùng mɯ̀ɯn** หนึ่ง หมื่น *one ten thousand*.

5.2 Ordinal numbers

In order to make ordinal numbers, we just need to place the prefix **thîi** ที่ before the number.

1st	thîi-nùng	ที่ หนึ่ง
2nd	thîi-sɔ̌ɔng	ที่ สอง
3rd	thîi-sǎam	ที่ สาม
4th	thîi-sìi	ที่ สี่
...		
24th	thîi-yîi-sìp-sìi	ที่ ยี่ สิบ สี่
etc.		

When talking about dates, we need to place **wan** วัน *day* before the date.

wan thîi-sɔ̌ɔng วัน ที่ สอง + name of the month means the second day of that month.

In English, we can say *the first of October;* in Thai, it becomes **wan thîi-nùng tùlaa-khom** วัน ที่ หนึ่ง ตุลา คม *day first October.*

thîi ที่ also has many other meanings such as *at, on, to, that, which, who, place, area*, etc. **thîi** ที่ is a multi-functional word.

Chapter 6

24-hour clock

24-hour clock time is expressed by **number** + **naalíkaa** นาฬิกา *o'clock, watch.*

We give here the normal clock time used in speaking on the right hand side for comparison.

Telling the clock time in Thai is quite special. We shall here introduce the 24-hour Thai clock time, which is similar to the Western
24-clock time.

It is simple and logical. We shall also compare it with the speaking
style, which is different. The difficulty is that Thais don't use the
24-hour clock time while communication with each other.

They will certainly understand you if you tell the time using the
24-hour clock. It is normally used in time tables and other official
situations. So, it is useful to know both.

6.1   Morning time

6.2   Afternoon time

6.3   Evening time

6.4   Night time

**6.5   Expressing minutes when using
         naalíkaa นาฬิกา o'clock**

6.1 Morning time

	24-hour clock	Speaking style
06:00	hòk naalíkaa	hòk moong tʃáu
	หก นาฬิกา	หก โมง เช้า (6.00 a.m.)
07:00	tsèt naalíkaa	tsèt moong tʃáu
	เจ็ด นาฬิกา	เจ็ด โมง เช้า (7.00 a.m.)
08:00	pɛ̀ɛt naalíkaa	pɛ̀ɛt moong tʃáu
	แปด นาฬิกา	แปด โมง เช้า (8.00 a.m.)
09:00	kâau naalíkaa	kâau moong tʃáu
	เก้า นาฬิกา	เก้า โมง เช้า (9.00 a.m.)
10:00	sìp naalíkaa	sìp moong tʃáu
	สิบ นาฬิกา	สิบ โมง เช้า (10.00 a.m.)
11:00	sìp èt naalíkaa	sìp èt moong tʃáu
	สิบ เอ็ด นาฬิกา	สิบ เอ็ด โมง เช้า (11.00 a.m.)
12:00	sìp sɔ̌ɔng naalíkaa	thîiang wan
	สิบ สอง นาฬิกา	เที่ยง วัน (Noon 12.00 p.m.)

6.2 Afternoon time

	24-hour clock	Speaking style
13:00	sìp sǎam naalíkaa	bàai moong
	สิบ สาม นาฬิกา	บ่าย โมง (1.00 p.m.)
14:00	sìp sìi naalíkaa	bàai sɔ̌ɔng moong
	สิบ สี่ นาฬิกา	บ่าย สอง โมง (2.00 p.m.)
15:00	sìp hâa naalíkaa	bàai sǎam moong
	สิบ ห้า นาฬิกา	บ่าย สาม โมง (3.00 p.m.)
16:00	sìp hòk naalíkaa	bàai sìi moong
	สิบ หก นาฬิกา	บ่าย สี่ โมง (4.00 p.m.)
17:00	sìp tsèt naalíkaa	hâa moong yen
	สิบ เจ็ด นาฬิกา	ห้า โมง เย็น (5.00 p.m.)
18:00	sìp pɛ̀ɛt naalíkaa	hòk moong yen
	สิบ แปด นาฬิกา	หก โมง เย็น (6.00 p.m.)

6.3 Evening time

	24-hour clock	Speaking style
19:00	**sìp kâau naalíkaa** สิบ เก้า นาฬิกา	**nùng thûm** หนึ่ง ทุ่ม (7.00 p.m.)
20:00	**yîi sìp naalíkaa** ยี่ สิบ นาฬิกา	**sɔ̌ɔng thûm** สอง ทุ่ม (8.00 p.m.)
21:00	**yîi sìp èt naalíkaa** ยี่ สิบ เอ็ด นาฬิกา	**sǎam thûm** สาม ทุ่ม (9.00 p.m.)
22:00	**yîi sìp sɔ̌ɔng naalíkaa** ยี่ สิบ สอง นาฬิกา	**sìi thûm** สี่ ทุ่ม (10.00 p.m.)
23:00	**yîi sìp sǎam naalíkaa** ยี่ สิบ สาม นาฬิกา	**hâa thûm** ห้า ทุ่ม (11.00 p.m.)
24:00	**yîi sìp sìi naalíkaa** ยี่ สิบ สี่ นาฬิกา	**thîiang khɯɯn** เที่ยง คืน *midnight* (12.00 a.m.)

6.4 Night time

	24-hour clock	Speaking style
00:00	**sǔun naalíkaa** ศูนย์ นาฬิกา	**thîiang khɯɯn** เที่ยง คืน *midnight* (12.00 a.m.)
01:00	**nùng naalíkaa** หนึ่ง นาฬิกา	**tii nùng** ตี หนึ่ง (1.00 a.m.)
02:00	**sɔ̌ɔng naalíkaa** สอง นาฬิกา	**tii sɔ̌ɔng** ตี สอง (2.00 a.m.)
03:00	**sǎam naalíkaa** สาม นาฬิกา	**tii sǎam** ตี สาม (3.00 a.m.)
04:00	**sìi naalíkaa** สี่ นาฬิกา	**tii sìi** ตี สี่ (4.00 a.m.)
05:00	**hâa naalíkaa** ห้า นาฬิกา	**tii hâa** ตี ห้า (5.00 a.m.)
06:00	**hòk naalíkaa** หก นาฬิกา	**hòk moong tʃáu** หก โมง เช้า (6.00 a.m.)

6.5 Expressing minutes when using naalíkaa นาฬิกา *o'clock*

number + **naalíkaa** นาฬิกา *o'clock* + **number** + **naathii** นาที *minutes*

00:01	**sǔun naalíkaa nùng naathii** ศูนย์ นาฬิกา หนึ่ง นาที (12.01 a.m.)
02:10	**sɔ̌ɔng naalíkaa sìp naathii** สอง นาฬิกา สิบ นาที (2.10 a.m.)
07:50	**tsèt naalíkaa hâa sìp naathii** เจ็ด นาฬิกา ห้า สิบ นาที (7.50 a.m.)
12:30	**sìp sɔ̌ɔng naalíkaa sǎam sìp naathii** สิบ สอง นาฬิกา สาม สิบ นาที (12.30 p.m.)*
19:05	**sìp kâau naalíkaa hâa naathii** สิบ เก้า นาฬิกา ห้า นาที (7.05 p.m.)

* Note that while speaking, the term **khrûng** ครึ่ง *half* (thirty minutes) is commonly used to refer to the time period of 30 minutes. However, it cannot be used when expressing time with **naalíkaa** นาฬิกา *o'clock.* You must express it as **sǎam sìp naathii** สาม สิบ นาที *thirty minutes.*

So, 12.30 p.m. = **thîiang (wan) khrûng** เที่ยง (วัน) ครึ่ง must be expressed as: **sìp sɔ̌ɔng naalíkaa sǎam sìp naathii** สิบ สอง นาฬิกา สาม สิบ นาที

There is an extensive review of expressing time when speaking in the book (chapter 17): *Learning Thai with Original Thai Words* (ISBN 978-952-6651-43-9)

◊

Chapter 7

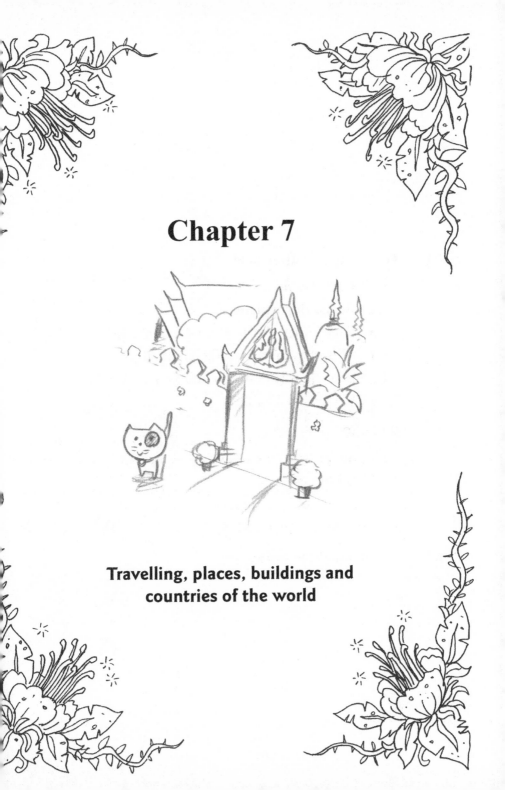

Travelling, places, buildings and countries of the world

7.1 Travelling and directions

7.1.1 Cars, trains...

thaang bòk	ทางบก	*by land*
rót	รถ	*car*
rót-yon	รถยนต์	*car*
rót-thɛ́k-sîi	รถ แท็กซี่	*taxi*
rót-mee	รถเมล์	*bus*
rót-bát	รถบัส	*bus*
rót-fai	รถ ไฟ	*train*
rót-fai tâi-din	รถ ไฟ ใต้ ดิน	*subway*
mɔɔtɔɔsai	มอเตอร์ไซค์	*motorcycle*
tsàk-kràyaan	จักรยาน	*bicycle*

7.1.2 Boats, ships, plains...

thaang náam	ทาง น้ำ	*by sea, by boat*
rɨa	เรือ	*boat, ship*
thaang aakàat	ทาง อากาศ	*by air*
khrûang-bin	เครื่อง บิน	*airplane*

7.1.3 Some other words related to traveling

tŭua	ตั๋ว	*ticket*
tŭua-thîiau-diiau	ตั๋ว เที่ยว เดียว	*one-way ticket*
tŭua-pai-klàp	ตั๋ว ไป กลับ	*round-trip ticket*
năngsɨ̆ɨ dɔɔn-thaang	หนังสือ เดิน ทาง	*passport*
phaasàpɔ̀ɔt	พาสปอร์ต	*passport*
wiisâa	วีซ่า	*visa*
ngən	เงิน	*money*
bàt-khreedìt	บัตร เครดิต	*credit card*
tûu ee-thii-em	ตู้ เอ ที เอ็ม	*ATM machine*

àttraa lɛ̂ɛk-plìian	อัตรา แลก เปลี่ยน	*exchange rate*
lɛ̂ɛk-plìian ngən	แลก เปลี่ยน เงิน	*money exchange*
phɛ̌ɛn-thîi	แผน ที่	*map*
kràpǎu	กระเป๋า	*bag*
kràpǎu dəən-thaang	กระเป๋า เดิน ทาง	*suitcase*
nák-thɔ̂ɔng-thîiau	นัก ท่อง เที่ยว	*tourist*
pràtuu thaang-ɔ̀ɔk	ประตู ทาง ออก	*exit gate*
tʃâu rót	เช่า รถ	*renting a car*
khěm-khàt níráphai	เข็ม ขัด นิรภัย	*seat belt*
bɔɔríkaan	บริการ	*service*
roong-rɛɛm	โรง แรม	*hotel*
ubàtihèet	อุบัติเหตุ	*accident*

7.1.4 This way, that way, left, right, etc.

thaang	ทาง	*way, path, route*
sáai	ซ้าย	*left*
khwǎa	ขวา	*right*
thaang sáai	ทาง ซ้าย	*on the left*
thaang khwǎa	ทาง ขวา	*on the right*
thaang nǎi	ทาง ไหน	*which way*
thaang níi	ทาง นี้	*this way*
thaang nán	ทาง นั้น	*that way*
thaang nóon	ทาง โน้น	*that way* (further)
thaang khâu	ทาง เข้า	*way in, entrance*
thaang ɔ̀ɔk	ทาง ออก	*way out, exit*
thaang ɔ̂ɔm	ทาง อ้อม	*detour*
thaang lát	ทาง ลัด	*shortcut*
thaang lǔuang	ทาง หลวง	*highway*

thaang dùuan	ทาง ด่วน	*expressway*
thaang tan	ทาง ตัน	*dead end*
thaang yɛ̂ɛk	ทาง แยก	*intersection* (traffic)
thaang nai*	ทาง ใน	*way in, meditation*
sǎam yɛ̂ɛk	สาม แยก	*3-way intersection* (traffic)
sìi yɛ̂ɛk	สี่ แยก	*4-way intersection* (traffic)

* Meditation is a Buddhist term. There are more words for *meditation,* mainly borrowed from Pali/Sanskrit such as **sàmaathí** สมาธิ *meditation, concentration.*

7.1.5 Directions (Points of compass)

tàwan	ตะวัน	*sun*
nǔua	เหนือ	*north*
tâi	ใต้	*south*
tàwan-ɔ̀ɔk	ตะวัน ออก	*east*
tàwan-tòk	ตะวัน ตก	*west*
tàwan ɔ̀ɔk tʃĭiang nǔua	ตะวัน ออก เฉียง เหนือ	*northeast*
tàwan ɔ̀ɔk tʃĭiang tâi	ตะวัน ออก เฉียง ใต้	*southeast*
tàwan tòk tʃĭiang nǔua	ตะวัน ตก เฉียง เหนือ	*northwest*
tàwan tòk tʃĭiang tâi	ตะวัน ตก เฉียง ใต้	*southwest*

7.1.6 Regions in Thailand

phâak	ภาค	*region*
phâak klaang	ภาค กลาง	*Central region*
phâak nǔua	ภาค เหนือ	*Nothern region*
phâak tâi	ภาค ใต้	*Southern region*
phâak tàwan ɔ̀ɔk	ภาค ตะวัน ออก	*Eastern region*
phâak tàwan tòk	ภาค ตะวัน ตก	*Western region*
phâak iisǎan	ภาค อีสาน (Isan)	*Northeastern region*

7.2 Buildings and places

7.2.1 Shops, stores, booths

ráan	ร้าน	*shop, store*
ráan-kaafɛɛ	ร้าน กาแฟ	*coffee shop*
ráan-aahǎan	ร้าน อาหาร	*restaurant*
ráan-nǎngsɯ̌ɯ	ร้าน หนังสือ	*bookstore*
ráan-sák-rîit	ร้าน ซัก รีด	*laundry*
ráan-khǎai-yaa	ร้าน ขาย ยา	*pharmacy, drugstore*
ráan-tàt-phǒm	ร้าน ตัด ผม	*barbershop*
ráan-tàt-sɯ̂ɯa	ร้าน ตัด เสื้อ	*tailor's shop*
ráan-khǎai-sɯ̂ɯa-phâa	ร้าน ขาย เสื้อ ผ้า	*clothes shop*

7.2.2 Buildings

roong	โรง	*building, house*
roong-riian	โรง เรียน	*school*
roong-rɛɛm	โรง แรม	*hotel*
roong-ngaan	โรง งาน	*factory*
roong-lákhɔɔn	โรง ละคร	*theater*
roong-phim	โรง พิมพ์	*printing house*
roong-rót	โรง รถ	*garage*
roong-nǎng	โรง หนัง	*movie theater*
roong-pháyaabaan	โรง พยาบาล	*hospital*

7.2.3 Some common places

bâan	บ้าน	*house, home*
wát	วัด	*temple*
bòot	โบสถ์	*church*
praasàat	ปราสาท	*castle*

anúsăawárii	อนุสาวรีย์	*monument*
sŭuan	สวน	*garden*
sŭuan-săathaaráná	สวน สาธารณะ	*public park*
sămnák-ngaan	สำนักงาน	*office*
wíttháyaalai	วิทยาลัย	*college*
máhăa-wíttháyaalai	มหา วิทยาลัย	*university*
praisànii	ไปรษณีย์	*post office*
thánaakhaan	ธนาคาร	*bank*
hɔ̂ng-sàmùt	ห้อง สมุด	*library*
baa	บาร์	*bar*
hɔ̂ng-náam	ห้อง น้ำ	*toilet*
hâang	ห้าง	*shop, store, firm*
tàlàat	ตลาด	*market*

7.2.4 Stations, airports, etc.

sàthăanii	สถานี	*station*
sàthăanii khŏn sòng	สถานี ขน ส่ง	*bus station*
sàthăanii-rót-fai	สถานี รถ ไฟ	*railway station*
sàthăanii MRT*	สถานี MRT	*subway station*
sàthăanii BTS*	สถานี BTS	*sky train station*
sàthăanii-tamrùuat	สถานี ตำรวจ	*police station*
sànăam	สนาม	*field, ground*
sànăam-bin	สนาม บิน	*airport*
sànăam-kiilaa	สนาม กีฬา	*sport stadium*

* Sky train in Bangkok is commonly know as BTS. It also has a Thai name **rót-fai-fáa** รถ ไฟ ฟ้า *sky train*. It is seldom used, however. Subway is known as MRT. The Thai name is **rót-tâi-din** รถ ใต้ ดิน subway.

7.3. Countries of the world

Note that **pràthêet** ประเทศ *country, nation, state* is normally placed before the name of the country to express the fact that it is an independent state.

7.3.1 Far East/Asia

pràthêet-bruunai	ประเทศ บรูไน	*Brunei*
khàmĕen*	เขมร	*Cambodia*
pràthêet-kamphuutʃaa	ประเทศ กัมพูชา	*Cambodia*
pràthêet-tsiin	ประเทศ จีน	*China*
hɔ̂ɔng-kong*	ฮ่องกง	*Hong Kong*
pràthêet-indooniisiia	ประเทศ อินโดนีเซีย	*Indonesia*
pràthêet-yîipùn	ประเทศ ญี่ปุ่น	*Japan*
pràthêet-laau	ประเทศ ลาว	*Laos*
pràthêet-maaleesiia	ประเทศ มาเลเซีย	*Malaysia*
pràthêet-miianmaa	ประเทศ เมียนมา	*Myanmar*
pràthêet-kaulĭi-nŭa	ประเทศ เกาหลีเหนือ	*North Korea*
pràthêet-fílíppin	ประเทศ ฟิลิปปินส์	*Philippines*
pràthêet-sĭngkhápoo	ประเทศ สิงคโปร์	*Singapore*
pràthêet-kaulĭi-tâi	ประเทศ เกาหลีใต้	*South Korea*
pràthêet-tâiwăn	ประเทศ ไต้หวัน	*Taiwan*
mɯɯang-thai*	เมือง ไทย	*Thailand*
pràthêet-thai	ประเทศ ไทย	*Thailand*
pràthêet-wîiatnaam	ประเทศ เวียดนาม	*Vietnam*

* The term **khàmĕen** เขมร is also often used to mean Cambodia.

* Hong Kong **hɔ̂ɔng-kong** ฮ่องกง *Hong Kong* is no longer an independent country.

* The term **mɯɯang-thai** เมือง ไทย is also often used to mean Thailand.

7.3.2 Other Asian countries

pràthêet-ɔ̀ɔttreeliia	ประเทศ ออสเตรเลีย	*Australia*
pràthêet-bangkhlaathêet	ประเทศ บังคลาเทศ	*Bangladesh*
pràthêet-indiia	ประเทศ อินเดีย	*India*
pràthêet-neepaan	ประเทศ เนปาล	*Nepal*
pràthêet-niusiilɛɛn	ประเทศ นิวซีแลนด์	*New Zealand*
pràthêet-paakìisathǎan	ประเทศ ปากีสถาน	*Pakistan*
pràthêet-srǐilangkaa	ประเทศ ศรีลังกา	*Sri Lanka*

7.3.3 Middle East

pràthêet-iiyìp	ประเทศ อียิปต์	*Egypt*
pràthêet-iràan	ประเทศ อิหร่าน	*Iran*
pràthêet-irák	ประเทศ อิรัก	*Iraq*
pràthêet-ìtsàraa-eeu	ประเทศ อิสราเอล	*Israel*
pràthêet-khuuwèet	ประเทศ คูเวต	*Kuwait*
pràthêet-líbiia	ประเทศ ลิเบีย	*Libya*
pràthêet-turakii	ประเทศ ตุรกี	*Turkey*
pràthêet-saaudì-aarabiia	ประเทศ ซาอุดิ อาระเบีย	*Saudi Arabia*

7.3.4 Europe

pràthêet-ɔ̀ɔttriia	ประเทศ ออสเตรีย	*Austria*
pràthêet-beenyîiam	ประเทศ เบลเยี่ยม	*Belgium*
pràthêet-deenmàak	ประเทศ เดนมาร์ก	*Denmark*
pràthêet-angkrìt	ประเทศ อังกฤษ	*England*
pràthêet-finlɛɛn	ประเทศ ฟินแลนด์	*Finland*
pràthêet-fàràngsèet	ประเทศ ฝรั่งเศส	*France*
pràthêet-yɔ̀ɔraman	ประเทศ เยอรมัน	*Germany*
pràthêet-ailɛɛn	ประเทศ ไอซ์แลนด์	*Iceland*

pràthêet-ìtaalîi	ประเทศ อิตาลี	Italy
pràthêet-neethɔ̀ɔlɛɛn	ประเทศ เนเธอร์แลนด์	Netherlands
pràthêet-nɔɔwee	ประเทศ นอร์เวย์	Norway
pràthêet-poolɛɛn	ประเทศ โปแลนด์	Poland
pràthêet-prootukèet	ประเทศ โปรตุเกส	Portugal
pràthêet-rátsiia	ประเทศ รัสเซีย	Russia
pràthêet-sàpeen	ประเทศ สเปน	Spain
pràthêet-sàwiideen	ประเทศ สวีเดน	Sweden
pràthêet-sàwítsɔɔlɛɛn	ประเทศ สวิตเซอร์แลนด์	Switzerland
sàhàrâat-tʃaa-anaatsàk*	สหราช อาณาจักร	United Kingdom

* The term **sàhàrâat-tʃaa-anaatsàk** สหราช อาณาจักร *United Kingdom*
is really not a country, but a group of countries.

7.3.5 America

pràthêet-aatseentìnâa	ประเทศ อาร์เจนตินา	Argentina
pràthêet-khɛɛnaadaa	ประเทศ แคนาดา	Canada
pràthêet-tʃǐlii	ประเทศ ชิลี	Chile
pràthêet-khoolambiia	ประเทศ โคลัมเบีย	Colombia
pràthêet-khɔ́ɔt-taaríkâa	ประเทศ คอสตาริกา	Costa Rica
pràthêet-khiubaa	ประเทศ คิวบา	Cuba
pràthêet-braasin	ประเทศ บราซิล	Brazil
pràthêet-méksíkoo	ประเทศ เม็กซิโก	Mexico
pràthêet-paanaamaa	ประเทศ ปานามา	Panama
pràthêet-peeruu	ประเทศ เปรู	Peru
pràthêet-pəətooríkôo	ประเทศ เปอร์โตริโก	Puerto Rico
pràthêet-weeneesuueelâa	ประเทศ เวเนซูเอลา	Venezuela
pràthêet-ameeríkaa*	ประเทศ อเมริกา	USA, America
sàhàrát ameeríkaa	สหรัฐ อเมริกา	United States of America

* The term **pràthêet-ameeríkaa** ประเทศ อเมริกา *America* is also often used to mean United States of America, USA.

7.3.6 Africa

pràthêet-ɛɛntsiiriia	ประเทศ แอลจีเรีย	*Algeria*
pràthêet-khɔɔngkôo	ประเทศ คองโก	*Congo*
pràthêet-kheenyâa	ประเทศ เคนยา	*Kenya*
pràthêet-moorɔ́kkoo	ประเทศ โมร็อกโก	*Morocco*
pràthêet-naitsiiriia	ประเทศ ไนจีเรีย	*Nigeria*
pràthêet-ɛ́ɛfríkaa-tâi	ประเทศ แอฟริกา ใต้	*South Africa*
pràthêet-thɛɛnsaaniia	ประเทศ แทนซาเนีย	*Tanzania*
pràthêet-tuunísiia	ประเทศ ตูนิเซีย	*Tunisia*
pràthêet-sɛɛmbiia	ประเทศ แซมเบีย	*Zambia*

Chapter 8

Names of some common animals and insects

máa	ม้า	*horse*
măa	หมา	*dog* (borrowed from Chinese)
sùnák	สุนัข	*dog* (borrowed from Pali/Sanskrit)
măa-pàa	หมา ป่า	*wolf*
máa-laai	ม้า ลาย	*zebra*
mɛɛu	แมว	*cat*
nŭu	หนู	*mouse, rat*
kài	ไก่	*chicken*
wuua	วัว	*cow*
kɛ̀	แกะ	*sheep*
kràrɔ́ɔk	กระรอก	*squirrel*
kràtàai	กระต่าย	*rabbit*
tʃáang	ช้าง	*elephant*
sŭua	เสือ	*tiger*
mĭi	หมี	*bear*
sĭng-too	สิงโต	*lion*
tsîng-tsɔ́ɔk	จิ้งจอก	*fox*
ling	ลิง	*monkey*
laa	ลา	*donkey*
ùut	อูฐ	*camel*
yiiráap	ยีราฟ	*giraffe*
málɛɛng	แมลง	*insect*
málɛɛng-wan	แมลง วัน	*fly*
málɛɛng-sàap	แมลง สาบ	*insect*
phûng	ผึ้ง	*bee*
yung	ยุง	*mosquito*
tsîng-tsòk	จิ้งจก	*lizard*
mót	มด	*ant*

Chapter 9

Foods, drinks and spices

Note that some words have been borrowed from other languages. This is the case particularly with the names of some drinks and desserts.

9.1 Some common Thai foods

aahăan	อาหาร	*food*
khâau	ข้าว	*rice*
khâau-phàt	ข้าว ผัด	*fried rice*
khâau-phàt-kûng	ข้าว ผัด กุ้ง	*fried rice with shrimp*
khâau-sŭuai	ข้าว สวย	*steamed rice*
khâau-nĭiau	ข้าว เหนียว	*sticky rice*
khâau-tôm	ข้าว ต้ม	*rice porridge*
kŭuai-tĭiau	ก๋วย เตี๋ยว	*noodles*
bàmìi	บะหมี่	*Chinese egg noodles*
phàt-thai	ผัด ไทย	*fried noodles*
sômtam	ส้มตำ	*papaya salad*
khànŏm-pang	ขนม ปัง	*bread*
puu	ปู	*crab*
plaa	ปลา	*fish*
plaa-mùk	ปลา หมึก	*squid*
kûng	กุ้ง	*prawn*
hɔ̆ɔi-naang-rom	หอย นาง รม	*oyster*
kài	ไก่	*chicken*
khài	ไข่	*egg*
khài-tsiiau	ไข่ เจียว	*omelet*
pèt	เป็ด	*duck*
hàan	ห่าน	*goose*
nɯ́a-kɛ̀	เนื้อ แกะ	*mutton*
nɯ́a-wuua	เนื้อ วัว	*beef*
mŭu	หมู	*pork*
hɛɛm	แฮม	*ham*

9.2 Vegetables, nuts, etc.

mákhǔa-thêet	มะเขือ เทศ	*tomato*
mákhǔa	มะเขือ	*eggplant*
man-fàràng	มัน ฝรั่ง	*potato*
tɛɛng-kwaa	แตง กวา	*cucumber*
tɛɛng-moo	แตง โม	*watermelon*
fák-thɔɔng	ฟัก ทอง	*pumpkin*
kàlàm-plii	กะหล่ำ ปลี	*cabbage*
kàlàm-dɔ̀ɔk	กะหล่ำ ดอก	*cauliflower*
brɔ̀k-khoolîi	บร็อคโคลี่	*broccoli*
khɛɛ-rɔ̀ɔt	แคร์รอต	*carrot*
khâau-phôot	ข้าว โพด	*corn*
hèt	เห็ด	*mushroom*
hǔua-hɔ̌ɔm	หัว หอม	*onion*
anmɔ̂ɔn	อัลมอนด์	*almond*
thùua	ถั่ว	*bean*
thùua-lǔang	ถั่ว เหลือง	soy *bean*
thùua-ngɔ̂ɔk	ถั่ว งอก	*bean sprout*
thùua-lísǒng	ถั่ว ลิสง	*peanut*
thùua-khǐiau	ถั่ว เขียว	*mung bean*

9.3 Fruits

klûuai	กล้วย	*banana*
ɛ́ɛppôn	แอปเปิ้ล	*apple*
sôm	ส้ม	*orange*
sôm-tsiin	ส้ม จีน	*tangerine*
sôm-oo	ส้ม โอ	*pomelo*
angùn	องุ่น	*grape*

mánaau	มะนาว	*lemon*
awookhaadôo	อะโวคาโด้	*avocado*
mákɔ̀ɔk	มะกอก	*olive*
mámûuang	มะม่วง	*mango*
khɛɛntaalúup	แคนตาลูป	*cantaloupe*
sàppàrót	สับปะรด	*pineapple*
máphráau	มะพร้าว	*coconut*
thúriian	ทุเรียน	*durian*
fàràng	ฝรั่ง	*guava*
líntsìi	ลิ้นจี่	*lychee*
kiiwîi	กีวี	*kiwi*
thápthim	ทับทิม	*pomegranate*
khànŭn	ขนุน	*jack fruit*
sǎuwárót	เสาวรส	*passion fruit*
mangkhút	มังคุด	*mangosteen*
lamyai	ลำไย	*longan*
laangsàat	ลางสาด	*langsat*
lɔɔngkɔɔng	ลองกอง	*longkong*
mákhǎam	มะขาม	*tamarind*
ngɔ́	เงาะ	*rambutan*

9.4 Drinks

náam	น้ำ	*water*
nám-khĕng	น้ำ แข็ง	*ice*
nám-rɛ̂ɛ	น้ำ แร่	*mineral water*
nám-sôm	น้ำ ส้ม	*orange juice*
nám-ɛ́ɛppɔ̂n	น้ำ แอปเปิ้ล	*apple juice*
kaafɛɛ	กาแฟ	*coffee*

nom	นม	*milk*
tʃaa	ชา	*tea*
biia	เบียร์	*beer*
waai	ไวน์	*wine*

9.5 Desserts

khànǒm	ขนม	*candy, sweets*
khànǒm-thai	ขนม ไทย	*Thai dessert*
khànǒm-phaai	ขนม พาย	*pie*
khâau-nǐiau-dam	ข้าว เหนียว ดำ	*black rice pudding*
khâau-nǐiau-mámûuang	ข้าว เหนียว มะม่วง	*sticky rice/mango*
klûuai tʃ ̂uam	กล้วย เชื่อม	*banana stewed in syrup*
klûuai bùuat-tʃii	กล้วย บวดชี	*banana in coconut milk*
sǎng-khàyǎa	สังขยา	*coconut custard*
tʃ ɔ́kkoolét	ช็อกโกแลต	*chocolate*
khúkkîi	คุกกี้	*cookies*
khéek	เค้ก	*cake*
aisàkhriim	ไอศกรีม	*ice-cream*
yɛɛm	แยม	*jam*

9.6 Spices

nám-plaa	น้ำ ปลา	*fish sauce*
phrík	พริก	*chili*
phrík-nám-plaa	พริก น้ำ ปลา	*fish sauce with chili*
phrík-thai	พริก ไทย	*pepper*
sɔ́ɔt-mákhǔathêet	ซอส มะเขือ เทศ	*ketchup*
kràthiiam	กระเทียม	*garlic*
nám-taan	น้ำ ตาล	*sugar*
nám-mákhǎam pìiak	น้ำ มะขาม เปียก	*tamarind sauce*

klɯa	เกลือ	*salt*
mánaau	มะนาว	*lime, lemon*
sàránὲε	สะระแหน่	*peppermint*
khǐng	ขิง	*ginger*
sɔ́ɔt-hɔ̌ɔi naang-rom	ซอส หอย นางรม	*oyster sauce*
òptʃəəi	อบเชย	*cinnamon*
phǒng-kàrìi	ผง กะหรี่	*curry powder*

Chapter 10

Health & personal items

10.1   Some common health vocabulary

10.2   Not feeling well

10.3   Common diseases

10.4   To heal illnesses

10.5   Personal items

10.1 Some common health vocabulary

ai	ไอ	*to cough*
phέε	แพ้	*to be allergic*
khan	คัน	*to itch*
buuam	บวม	*to swell*
hŭua-tsai-waai	หัว ใจ วาย	*to have heart attack*
bàat-phlĕε	บาด แผล	*wound, cut*
láang phlĕε	ล้าง แผล	*to clean a wound*
ráksăa phlĕε	รักษา แผล	*to heal a wound*
phláattɔ̀ɔ	พลาสเตอร์	*bandage, plaster*
khĕm	เข็ม	*needle*
fãng-khĕm	ฝัง เข็ม	*acupuncture*
nûuat	นวด	*massage*
nûuat-phĕεn-thai	นวด แผน ไทย	*Thai massage*
wítaamin	วิตามิน	*vitamin*

10.2 Not feeling well

mâi sàbaai	ไม่ สบาย	*not feeling well*
pùuat	ปวด	*to ache*
pùuat-hŭua	ปวด หัว	*to have a headache*
pùuat-thɔ́ɔng	ปวด ท้อง	*to have a stomachache*
pùuat-fan	ปวด ฟัน	*to have toothache*
pùuat-lăng	ปวด หลัง	*to have a backache*
tsèp	เจ็บ	*to be hurt*
khon-tsèp	คน เจ็บ	*patient* (by accident)
bàat-tsèp	บาด เจ็บ	*to be injured, hurt*
tsèp-pùuai	เจ็บ ป่วย	*to be sick*
tsèp-pùuat	เจ็บ ปวด	*to have pain*

tsèp-khɔɔ	เจ็บ คอ	*to have pain in throat*
tsèp-tsai	เจ็บ ใจ	*to get hurt mentally (heartbroken)*
wàt	หวัด	*common cold*
khâi	ไข้	*fever*
khâi-wàt	ไข้ หวัด	*flu, cold*
pen-wàt	เป็น หวัด	*to have a cold*
pen-khâi	เป็น ไข้	*to have a fever*
pen-lom	เป็น ลม	*to feel dizzy*

10.3 Common diseases

rôok	โรค	*disease*
pen-rôok	เป็น โรค	*to have a disease*
pen-rôok-bau-wăn	เป็น โรค เบา หวาน	*to have diabetes*
pen-rôok-hŭua-tsai	เป็น โรค หัว ใจ	*to have a heart disease*
pen-rôok-máreng	เป็น โรค มะเร็ง	*to have cancer*
tìt	ติด	*to be addicted to*
tìt-tʃúa	ติด เชื้อ	*to catch an infection*
tìt-yaa	ติด ยา	*to be addicted to drugs*
tìt-bùrìi	ติด บุหรี่	*to be addicted to smoking*
tìt-lâu	ติด เหล้า	*to be an alcoholic*

10.4 To heal illnesses

ráksăa rôok	รักษา โรค	*to heal illness*
mɔ̆ɔ	หมอ	*doctor*
mɔ̆ɔ-fan	หมอ ฟัน	*dentist*
mɔ̆ɔ-phĭi	หมอ ผี	*witch doctor*
yaa	ยา	*medicine*
ráan-khăai-yaa	ร้าน ขาย ยา	*pharmacy, drugstore*

yaa-mét	ยา เม็ด	*tablet*
yaa-ɛ́ɛtphairin	ยา แอสไพริน	*aspirin*
yaa-kɛ̂ɛ-ai	ยา แก้ ไอ	*cough medicine*
tʃìit yaa	ฉีด ยา	*to inject*
yaa-nɔɔn-làp	ยา นอน หลับ	*sleeping pill*
yaa-kɛ̂ɛ-pùuat	ยา แก้ ปวด	*pain killer*
yaa-lót-khâi	ยา ลด ไข้	*medicine for fever*
yaa-sàmŭn-phrai	ยา สมุน ไพร	*herbal medicine*
yaa-khum (kamnə̀ət)	ยา คุม (กำเนิด)	*birth-control pills*
yaa-yɔ̀ɔt-taa	ยา หยอด ตา	*eye drops*
yaa-kɛ̂ɛ thɔ́ɔng-sĭia	ยา แก้ ท้อง เสีย	*medicine for diarrhea*
yaa-rábaai	ยา ระบาย	*laxative*
yaa-klɔ̀ɔm-pràsàat	ยา กล่อม ประสาท	*tranquilizer*
yaa-pàtì-tʃiiwáná	ยา ปฏิชีวนะ	*antibiotic*

10.5 Personal items

sàbùu	สบู่	*soap*
tʃɛɛmphuu	แชมพู	*shampoo*
pɛ̂ɛng	แป้ง	*powder*
lootʃân	โลชั่น	*lotion*
roon-ɔɔn	โรลออน	*deodorant*
phâa-anaamai	ผ้า อนามัย	*sanitary napkin, tampon*
fan	ฟัน	*tooth*
prɛɛng	แปรง	*brush*
prɛɛng-sĭi-fan	แปรง สี ฟัน	*toothbrush*
yaa-sĭi-fan	ยา สี ฟัน	*toothpaste*
prɛɛng fan	แปรง ฟัน	*to brush teeth*
máai-tsîm-fan	ไม้ จิ้ม ฟัน	*toothpick*

pùuat-fan	ปวด ฟัน	*to have a toothache*
fan-phù	ฟัน ผุ	*bad tooth*
phŏm	ผม	*hair*
wĭi	หวี	*comb*
wĭi phŏm	หวี ผม	*to comb*
tàt phŏm	ตัด ผม	*to cut hair*
ráan-tàt-phŏm	ร้าน ตัด ผม	*barbershop*
thîi-khâat-phŏm	ที่ คาด ผม	*hair band*
khriim-nûuat-phŏm	ครีม นวด ผม	*hair conditioner*
khrûuang-pàu-phŏm	เครื่อง เป่า ผม	*hair dryer*
phŏm-plɔɔm	ผม ปลอม	*wig, false hair*
lép	เล็บ	*nail*
thîi-tàt-lép	ที่ ตัด เล็บ	*nail clippers*
tàbai-lép	ตะไบ เล็บ	*nail file*
yaa-thaa-lép	ยา ทา เล็บ	*nail polish*
tham lép	ทำ เล็บ	*to trim nails*
sămaang	สำอาง	*to be good-looking*
khrûang-sămaang	เครื่อง สำอาง	*cosmetics*
tɛ̀ɛng-nâa	แต่ง หน้า	*to put on make-up*
foom-láang-nâa	โฟม ล้าง หน้า	*facial cleanser*
khriim-kan-dɛ̀ɛt	ครีม กัน แดด	*sunscreen*
lípsàtìk	ลิปสติก	*lipstick*
koon	โกน	*to shave*
mîit-koon	มีด โกน	*razor*
bai-mîit-koon	ใบ มีด โกน	*razor blade*
kankrai	กรรไกร	*scissors*
khĕm-klàt	เข็ม กลัด	*safety pin*

Chapter 11

Adjectives

One particular feature of Thai adjectives is that they can also play the role of a verb and an adverb.

Generally, adjectives in Thai are easy to identify since they are concerned with "what kind". Therefore, we normally place the verb "to be" in front of an adjective in English. In addition, they can be used as adverbs.

11.1   General adjectives

11.2   Adjectives normally related to people and feelings

11.3   Adjectives describing quality, often used for things

11.4   Colours as adjectives

11.5   Camparison of adjectives

11.1 General adjectives

Examples:

> thîi nîi *nâa-bùua* mâak   ที่ นี่ น่า เบื่อ มาก
> place this *nâa-boring* very – *It is very boring here.*

phɔɔ	พอ	*to be enough*
tem	เต็ม	*to be full* (general)
dii	ดี	*to be good*
mâi dii	ไม่ ดี	*to be bad, not good*
yɛ̂ɛ	แย่	*to be bad, terrible*
leeu	เลว	*to be bad, evil*
sǔung	สูง	*to be tall*
nàk	หนัก	*to be heavy*
sànùk	สนุก	*to be fun*
sàdùuak	สะดวก	*to be convenient, comfortable*
bùua	เบื่อ	*to be bored*
plɛ̀ɛk	แปลก	*to be strange, weird*
too	โต	*to be big, large, a grown up*

11.2 Adjectives normally related to people and feelings

Examples:

> phûu-yǐng khon nán *nâa-rák* ผู้ หญิง คน นั้น น่ารัก
> person-female person that *nâa-love* – *That girl is cute.*

im	อิ่ม	*to be full* (eating)
dii-tsai	ดี ใจ	*to be happy*
sùk	สุข	*to be happy, pleased*
sàbaai	สบาย	*to be well*

mâi sàbaai	ไม่ สบาย	*not to be well*
sǔuai	สวย	*to be beautiful*
nâa-rák	น่า รัก	*to be cute, pretty, attractive*
lɔ̀ɔ	หล่อ	*to be handsome, attractive*
aai	อาย	*to be shy*
kluua	กลัว	*to be scary*
kèng	เก่ง	*to be skilled, talented, efficient*
tʃàlàat	ฉลาด	*to be clever, smart*
yûng	ยุ่ง	*to be busy*
wâang	ว่าง	*to be free*
moo-hǒo	โมโห	*to be angry*
tsing	จริง	*to be honest, real*
nɛ̂ɛ	แน่	*to be sure, certain*

11.3 Adjectives describing quality, often used for things

Examples:

> aahǎan thai *arɔ̀i* mâak   อาหาร ไทย อร่อย มาก
> food thai *delicious* very – *Thai food is very delicious.*

arɔ̀i	อร่อย	*to be delicious*
phèt	เผ็ด	*to be spicy*
khem	เค็ม	*to be salty*
wǎan	หวาน	*to be sweet*
lék	เล็ก	*to be small*
yài	ใหญ่	*to be big*
sǔung	สูง	*to be tall*
nàk	หนัก	*to be heavy*
mâi nàk	ไม่ หนัก	*to be light, not to be heavy*

phɛɛng	แพง	*to be expensive*
thùuk	ถูก	*to be cheap, correct*
mài	ใหม่	*to be new*
klom	กลม	*to be round*
ngâai	ง่าย	*to be easy*
yâak	ยาก	*to be difficult*
rɔ́ɔn	ร้อน	*to be hot*
năau	หนาว	*to be cold*
yen	เย็น	*to be cool*
sĭia	เสีย	*to be spoiled*
nɔ́ɔi	น้อย	*to be few, not many*
reu	เร็ว	*to be fast*
ʧáa	ช้า	*to be slow*

11.4 Colours as adjectives

Examples:

> *sĭi-fáa* sŭuai thîi-sùt สี ฟ้า สวย ที่ สุด
> *colour-sky* beautiful that-most
> *The light blue is the most beautiful colour.*

sĭi-dam	สี ดำ	*to be black*
sĭi-khăau	สี ขาว	*to be white*
sĭi-dɛɛng	สี แดง	*to be red*
sĭi-lŭang	สี เหลือง	*to be yellow*
sĭi-nám-ngən	สี น้ำ เงิน	*to be dark blue*
sĭi-fáa	สี ฟ้า	*to be light blue (sky blue)*
sĭi-khĭiau	สี เขียว	*to be green*
sĭi-sôm	สี ส้ม	*to be orange (orange colour)*

sǐi-mûuang	สี ม่วง	*to be purple*
sǐi-tʃom-phuu	สี ชมพู	*to be pink*
sǐi-nám-taan	สี น้ำ ตาล	*to be brown (brown sugar colour)*
sǐi-thau	สี เทา	*to be gray*
sǐi-thɔɔng	สี ทอง	*to be golden (golden colour)*
sǐi-ngən	สี เงิน	*to be silver (silver colour)*

11.5 Comparative adjectives

For the complete review of comparative adjectives, refer to Chapter 20, page 183.

Chapter 12

Adverbs

There are many types of adverbs. Adverbs normally answer the question: how? how often? where? what way? to what degree? Adverbs make the meaning more clear and specific. They can modify adjectives, verbs and other adverbs.

Sometimes in Thai, it is not easy to make a distinction weather the adjective plays the role of a verb or an adverb. Hence, we must understand the meaning from the context. Normally, Thais don't think in terms of adverbs. So, we will follow the English adverb categories. That way we will be able to cover a good selection of some important words, which are used by Thais every day.

In Thai, with adverbs, we normally need a main verb in the sentence. With adjectives the main verb is not required since adjectives can play the role of a verb in the sentence.

12.1 *How?* (Adverbs of manner)

Adverbs of manner are very much related to adjectives. In English, adverbs are often formed by adding -ly at the end of an adjective.

In Thai, we can make adverbs of manner from adjectives by placing the helping verb **dâai** ได้ *can* in the front of most adjectives.

dâai ได้ + dii ดี   *to be good*   = *well*

dâai ได้ + sŭuai สวย   *to be beautiful*   = *beautifully*

dâai ได้ + ʧáa ช้า   *to be slow*   = *slowly*

dâai ได้ + reu เร็ว   *to be fast*   = *fast, quickly*

etc.

Examples:

> **1** kháu *dii* เขา ดี
> he *good* – *He is good.*

- Here **dii** ดี *good* is an adjective. An adjective answers the question *what kind.* When an adjective also plays the role of a verb, there is no need for another verb.

> **2** kháu khàp *dâai-dii* เขา ขับ ได้ ดี
> he drive *can-good* – *He drives well.*

- Here we added an action verb **khàp** ขับ *to drive* and placed the helping verb **dâai** ได้ *can* before the adjective **dii** ดี. Now, **dii** ดี *good* has become the adverb *well*. Adverbs of manner answer the question *how.*

> **3** kháu khàp *dii* เขา ขับ ดี
> he drive *good* – *He drives well.*

- We may also drop **dâai** ได้ *can* and the translation into English is still the same. The adverb in Thai is understood from the context.
- With some adjectives **dâai** ได้ cannot be used to form adverbs. They can be used directly either as adjectives or adverbs.

nàk	หนัก	*heavy, heavily*
kèng	เก่ง	*diligent, diligently*
ngâai	ง่าย	*easy, easily*

Similarly, in English we have a few words like that. *Fast* is one of them. It can be both an adjective and an adverb.

12.2 When? (Adverbs of time)

Adverbs of time answer the question *when*.

Adverbs of time are very important since they play a major role as far as Thai tenses are concerned.

12.2.1 Present time words

Examples:

> *dǐiau-níi* phǒm kin-khâau yùu เดี๋ยว นี้ ผม กิน ข้าว อยู่
> *moment-this* I eat-rice be – *Now, I am eating.*

dǐiau-níi	เดี๋ยว นี้	*now*
tɔɔn-níi	ตอน นี้	*now*
pàt-tsùban	ปัจจุบัน	*nowadays*
wan-níi	วัน นี้	*today*
aathít-níi	อาทิตย์ นี้	*this week*
dʉʉan-níi	เดือน นี้	*this month*
pii-níi	ปี นี้	*this year*
tʃáu-níi	เช้า นี้	*this morning*
khʉʉn-níi	คืน นี้	*tonight*

12.2.2 Past time words

Examples:

> *mɯ̂ɯa-kɔ̀ɔn* kháu khîi-aai mâak เมื่อ ก่อน เขา ขี้อาย มาก
> *when-before* he khîi-shy very – *Before, he was very shy.*

mɯ̂ɯa-waan	เมื่อวาน	*yesterday*
wan-waan	วันวาน	*day before yesterday*
wan-kɔ̀ɔn	วัน ก่อน	*the other day*
mɯ̂ɯa-khɯɯn	เมื่อ คืน	*last night*
aathít thîi-lɛ́ɛu	อาทิตย์ ที่ แล้ว	*last week*
dɯɯan thîi-lɛ́ɛu	เดือน ที่ แล้ว	*last month*
pii thîi-lɛ́ɛu	ปี ที่ แล้ว	*last year*
mɯ̂ɯa-kɔ̀ɔn	เมื่อ ก่อน	*before, previously*
lăai pii kɔ̀ɔn	หลาย ปี ก่อน	*many years ago*
tâng-tɛ̀ɛ	ตั้ง แต่	*since*

12.2.3 Future time words

Examples:

> *dɯɯan-nâa* tʃǎn tsà tɛ̀ɛng-ngaan เดือน หน้า ฉัน จะ แต่ง งาน
> *month-next* I will prepare-ceremony
> *I will get married next month.*

phrûng-níi	พรุ่ง นี้	*tomorrow*
márɯɯn-níi	มะรืน นี้	*day after tomorrow*
aathít-nâa	อาทิตย์ หน้า	*next week*
dɯɯan-nâa	เดือน หน้า	*next month*
pii-nâa	ปี หน้า	*next year*
ìik sɔ̌ɔng aathít	อีก สอง อาทิตย์	*two weeks from now*

| ìik săam dʉʉan | อีก สาม เดือน | *three months from now* |
| ìik sìi pii | อีก สี่ ปี | *four years from now* |

12.3 *How often?* (Adverbs of frequency)

Adverbs of frequency tell how often something happens. We use them a lot.

Examples:

> phŏm maa thîi níi *bɔ̀i-bɔ̀i* ผม มา ที่ นี่ บ่อยๆ
> I come place-this *often-often – I come here often.*

bɔ̀i, bɔ̀i-bɔ̀i	บ่อย, บ่อยๆ	*often*
sàmɔ̌ɔ	เสมอ	*always*
baang-khráng	บาง ครั้ง	*sometimes*
thammádaa	ธรรมดา	*normally*
pòkkàtì	ปกติ	*usually, normally*
pràtsam	ประจำ	*regularly*
mʉ̌ʉan-khəəi	เหมือน เคย	*as usual*
mâi khəəi	ไม่ เคย	*never*
mâi khɔ̂i	ไม่ ค่อย	*hardly*
tàlɔ̀ɔt-weelaa	ตลอด เวลา	*all the time*
tàlɔ̀ɔt-pai	ตลอด ไป	*forever*
tàlɔ̀ɔt-wan	ตลอด วัน	*all day long*
tàlɔ̀ɔt-khʉʉn	ตลอด คืน	*all night long*
tàlɔ̀ɔt-pii	ตลอด ปี	*all year round*
tàlɔ̀ɔt-maa	ตลอด มา	*all along, consistently*
tàlɔ̀ɔt-tʃiiwít	ตลอด ชีวิต	*throughout the life*
thúk-khráng	ทุก ครั้ง	*every time*
thúk-wan	ทุก วัน	*every day*

thúk-tʃáu	ทุก เช้า	*every morning*
thúk-yen	ทุก เย็น	*every evening*
thúk-aathít	ทุก อาทิตย์	*every week*
thúk-dɯɯan	ทุก เดือน	*every month*
thúk-pii	ทุก ปี	*every year*
thúk-khɯɯn	ทุก คืน	*every night*
aathít lá khráng	อาทิตย์ ละ ครั้ง	*once a week*
dɯɯan lá sɔ̌ɔng khráng	เดือน ละ สอง ครั้ง	*twice a month*
pii lá sǎam khráng	ปี ละ สาม ครั้ง	*three times a year*

12.4 *How many?* (Adverbs of quantity)

Adverbs of quantity tell more about the action. Adverbs of quantity indicate the amount of the action.

Adverbs of quantity are normally used with so called countable nouns. Therefore, adverbs of quantity often need to be used with a *classifier.*

Examples:

> **1** kháu mii rót *lǎai khan* เขา มี รถ หลาย คัน
> he have car *many vehicle – He has many cars.*

- Here we must use the classifier **khan** คัน with **lǎai** หลาย *many.* The meaning is the same or very similar as in the following sentences with **yɔ́** เยอะ *much, many* or **mâak** มาก *much, many.*

> **2** kháu mii rót *yɔ́* เขา มี รถ เยอะ
> he have car *many – He has many cars.*

- A classifier for a car is **khan** คัน *vehicle,* but with **yɔ́** เยอะ *much, many* it is dropped.

kháu mii rót *mâak* เขา มี รถ เยอะ มาก
he have car *many – He has many cars.*

- A classifier for a car is **khan** คัน *vehicle,* but with **mâak** มาก *much, many* it is dropped.

lăai	หลาย	*many*
baang	บาง	*some*
thúk	ทุก	*all*
thúk-thúk	ทุกๆ	*every, each*
yɔ́*	เยอะ	*many, much*
mâak*	มาก	*many*
nɔ́ɔi*	น้อย	*a little*

* These adverbs can be used without a classifier.

12.5 *How much? To what degree?* (Adverbs of degree)

Adverbs of degree tell more about the intensity of an action. Adverbs of degree are used in the similar manner as adverbs of quantity. Adverbs of degree indicate the intensity of the action while adverbs of quantity express the amount of the action. The distinction is very subtle.

Adverbs of degree are normally used with uncountable nouns. Adverbs of degree usually follow a verb or an adjective, and *are not used with a classifier.*

Examples:

kháu phûut *mâak* เขา พูด มาก
he speak *much – He speaks a lot.*

- **mâak** มาก *much* is used here as an *adverbs of degree*. **mâak** มาก *much* follows the verb **phûut** พูด *to speak*. The adverb of degree **mâak** มาก *much* modify the verb **phûut** พูด *to speak*.

phɔɔ	พอ	*enough*
nít-nɔ̀i	นิด หน่อย	*a little bit*
nɔ̀i	หน่อย	*a little*
tsang	จัง	*very*
mâak	มาก	*very, much, a lot*
bâang	บ้าง	*some, any*
tsing-tsing	จริงๆ	*really*
mâi khɔ̂i	ไม่ ค่อย	*hardly*
kùuap	เกือบ	*almost*
bau-bau	เบาๆ	*gently, softly*

12.6 *How certain?* (Adverbs of certainty)

Adverbs of certainty tell *how likely* an action or an event is going to take place. In Thai, adverbs of certainty are often placed at the end of the sentence, but some adverbs are placed before the action verb or at the beginning of the sentence.

Examples:

> **1** phǒm tsà pai *nɛ̂ɛ-nɔɔn* ผม จะ ไป แน่ นอน
> I will go *sure-sleep – I will go for sure.*

- In this sentence, adverbs of certainty **nɛ̂ɛ-nɔɔn** แน่ นอน *for sure, certainly* modifies the verb **pai** ไป *go*. It is placed at the end of the sentence.

> **2** phǒm *àat-tsà* pai ผม อาจ จะ ไป
> I *perhaps-will* go – *Perhaps, I will go.*

In this sentence, the adverbs of certainty **àat-tsà** อาจ จะ *perhaps, maybe* modifies the verb **pai** ไป *to go*. It is placed before the verb **pai** ไป *to go*.

nɛ̂ɛ-nɔɔn	แน่ นอน	*for sure, definitely, certainly*
khong-tsà	คง จะ	*perhaps*
àat-tsà	อาจ จะ	*maybe*
khuuan-tsà	ควร จะ	*should*
tɔ̂ng	ต้อง	*must*
tsing	จริง	*truly, really*
sùuan-mâak	ส่วน มาก	*mostly*
tʃát-tsɛ̂ɛng	ชัด แจ้ง	*clearly, obviously*
nǎi-nǎi	ไหนๆ	anyway

12.7 Where? What place? (Adverbs of place)

Under this heading we will list words which refer to a certain place or location. They tell us where something happens.

12.7.1 Here and there, anywhere, everywhere, somewhere, elsewhere, nowhere

Examples:

> tʃán yàak pai thîi *ɯ̀ɯn-ɯ̀ɯn* ฉัน อยาก ไป ที่ อื่นๆ
> I want go place *other-other – I want to go elsewhere!*

thîi-nîi	ที่ นี่	*here*
thîi-nân	ที่ นั่น	*there*
thîi nôon	ที่ โน่น	*over there*
thîi ɯ̀ɯn-ɯ̀ɯn	ที่ อื่นๆ	*elsewhere, somewhere else*
thúk-thîi	ทุก ที่	*everywhere*
thîi-nǎi	ที่ ไหน	*anywhere*

12.7.2 Outside, inside, downstairs, upstairs, in front of, behind, far, nearby, etc.

Examples:

> kháu yùu *khâang-bon* เขา อยู่ ข้าง บน
> he stay *side-above – He is upstairs.*

khâang-nɔ̂ɔk	ข้าง นอก	*outside*
khâang-nai	ข้าง ใน	*inside*
khâang-lâang	ข้าง ล่าง	*downstairs*
khâang-bon	ข้าง บน	*upstairs*
khâang-nâa	ข้าง หน้า	*in front of*
khâang-lăng	ข้าง หลัง	*behind*
klâi-klâi	ใกล้ๆ	*nearby*
klai	ไกล	*far*
tàang-pràthêet	ต่าง ประเทศ	*abroad, overseas*

12.8 Adverbs modifying adjectives

Often, we use adverbs to modify adjectives to tell more about an adjective.

Adverbs:	mâak	มาก	*much*
	kəən-pai	เกิน ไป	*too*
	tsang	จัง	*very much*
	nít-nɔ̀i	นิด หน่อย	*a bit*
	phɔɔ	พอ	*enough*

Examples:

> phûu-yĭng *sŭuai mâak* ผู้หญิง สวย มาก
> person-female *beautiful very – Girls are very beautiful.*

sŭuai mâak	สวย มาก	*very beautiful*
ʧáa mâak	ช้า มาก	*very slow*
reu mâak	เร็ว มาก	*very fast*
bùɯa mâak	เบื่อ มาก	*very boring*
nâa-rák tsang	น่า รัก จัง	*very pretty*
klai tsang	ไกล จัง	*very far*
kluua tsang	กลัว จัง	*very scary*
nàk kəən-pai	หนัก เกิน ไป	*too heavy*
yài kəən-pai	ใหญ่ เกิน ไป	*too big*
dii phɔɔ	ดี พอ	*good enough*
ʧàlàat phɔɔ	ฉลาด พอ	*intelligent enough*
sŭung phɔɔ	สูง พอ	*tall enough*
lék nít-nɔ̀i	เล็ก นิด หน่อย	*a little small*
aai nít-nɔ̀i	อาย นิด หน่อย	*a little shy*
yûng nít-nɔ̀i	ยุ่ง นิด หน่อย	*a little busy*

12.9 Adverbs modyfying adverbs

Often, we use adverbs to modify other adverbs to tell more about the adverb.

kəən-pai เกินไป *too* is a good example:

> yàa khàp *reu kəən-pai* อย่า ขับ เร็ว เกิน ไป
> don't drive *fast exceed-go – Don't drive too fast.*

- **reu** มาก เร็ว is used here as an adverb *fast, quickly.* The adverb **kəən-pai** เกิน ไป *too* tells more about driving fast, *too fast.*

reu kəən-pai	เร็ว เกิน ไป	*too fast, too soon*
ʧáa kəən-pai	ช้า เกิน ไป	*too slow*
mâak kəən-pai	หนัก เกิน ไป	*too much*

nɔ́ɔi kəən-pai	น้อย เกิน ไป	*too little*
bɔ̀i kəən-pai	บ่อย เกิน ไป	*too often*
klâi kəən-pai	ใกล้ เกิน ไป	*too close*
klai kəən-pai	ไกล เกิน ไป	*too far*

12.10 Adverbs made by doubling adjectives

Often adverbs can also be made by doubling an adjective.

Examples:

1   tham *bau-bau* dûuai   ทำ เบาๆ ด้วย
do *gentle-gently* also – *Please do it gently!*

2   kháu phûut *tʃát-tʃát*   เขา พูด ชัดๆ
he speak *clear-clear* – *He speaks clearly.*

sàbaai-sàbaai	สบายๆ	*well*
bau-bau	เบาๆ	*gently, softly*
tʃát-tʃát	ชัดๆ	*clearly*
nɛ̂ɛ-nɛ̂ɛ	แน่ๆ	*surely, definitely*
bɔ̀i-bɔ̀i	บ่อยๆ	*often*
etc.		

- Doubling an adjective is very common in Thai. That way we can place more emphasis on the action in question. Often, it also sounds better than using a single word.

12.11 Comparative adverbs

For the complete review of comparative adverbs, refer to Chapter 20, page 183.

◊

Chapter 13

Verbs

Commonly used *verbs* and **lέεu** แล้ว *already*

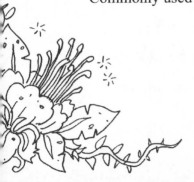

Here we would like to demonstrate how the time indicator **lɛ́ɛu** แล้ว *already* is connected to different types of verbs and Thai tenses.

Note that **lɛ́ɛu** แล้ว *already* is used with states and conditions or actions which can be changed. It is usually not used with universal truths or long term facts which cannot be changed.

Generally, verbs can be divided into two broad categories, state verbs and action verbs. In addition, we can divide each category into two groups. Then, we have four groups of verbs. They are:

1. Adjectives as state verbs
2. Common state verbs
3. Long term action verbs
4. Short term action verbs

This is important to understand since the type of verb we use may change the tense in Thai. Note also that adjectives in Thai can play the role of an adjective, verb or adverb.

In the following examples the English tense is normally either the present simple tense or the present continuous tense (action going on). With short term action verbs the tense is usually the present perfect tense (action completed).

13.1   **Adjectives as state verbs + lɛ́ɛu แล้ว *already***

13.2   **Other common state verbs + lɛ́ɛu แล้ว *already***

13.3   **Long term action verbs + lɛ́ɛu แล้ว *already***

13.4   **Short term action verbs + lɛ́ɛu แล้ว *already***

13.1 Adjectives as state verbs + lέεu แล้ว *already*

In Thai, adjectives can play the role of a verb. They are called state verbs. State verbs and **lέεu** แล้ว *already* usually constitute the *present simple tense* in English.

Examples:

> **1** *phɔɔ lέεu* พอ แล้ว
> *enough already – It is already enough. / It is enough now.*

- In this sentence, the adjective **phɔɔ** พอ *enough* + **lέεu** แล้ว *already* express the state which has been reached; it is true now.

- In English, we express this with the *present simple tense* (It is...).

> **2** khun *sǔuai lέεu* คุณ สวย แล้ว
> you *beautiful already*
> *You are already beautiful. / Now, you are beautiful.*

- In this sentence, the adjective **sǔuai** สวย *beautiful* + **lέεu** แล้ว *already* express the state which has been reached; it is true now.

- In English, we express this with the *present simple tense* (You are...).

- Sometimes, it is more natural to translate an adjective + **lέεu** แล้ว *already* as *now*.

Adjectives:

phɔɔ พอ   *to be enough*   + lέεu แล้ว= *to be enough now*

im อิ่ม   *to be full*   + lέεu แล้ว= *to be already full*

thùuk ถูก   *to be correct*   + lέεu แล้ว= *to be correct now*

moo-hǒo โมโห *to be angry* + lέεu แล้ว= *to be already angry*

too โต   *to be a grown up* + lέεu แล้ว= *to be already grown up*

sǔuai สวย *to be beautiful*   + lέεu แล้ว= *to be beautiful now*

- Sometimes, it is more natural to translate an adjective + **lέεu** แล้ว *already* as *now*.

13.2 Other common state verbs + lɛ́ɛu แล้ว *already*

State verbs describe a certain state. They do not express any action. Sometimes, in English, state verbs are called stative verbs. They usually refer to states of being, to emotions, to senses or to thoughts.

With state verbs the English tense normally is the *present simple tense*.

Examples:

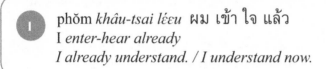

> **1** phǒm *khâu-tsai lɛ́ɛu* ผม เข้า ใจ แล้ว
> I *enter-hear already*
> *I already understand. / I understand now.*

- In this sentence, the verb **khâu-tsai** เข้า ใจ *to understand* + **lɛ́ɛu** แล้ว *already* express the state which has been reached; it is true now.

- In English, we express this with the *present simple tense* (I understand...).

> **2** tʃán *wái-tsai* kháu *lɛ́ɛu* ฉัน ไว้ ใจ เขา แล้ว
> I *keep-heart* he *already*
> *I trust him already. / I trust him now.*

- In this sentence, the verb **wái-tsai** ไว้ ใจ *to trust* + **lɛ́ɛu** แล้ว *already* express the state which has been reached; it is true now.

- In English, we express this with the *present simple tense* (I trust...)

State verbs:

khâu-tsai	เข้า ใจ	*to understand*	+ lɛ́ɛu แล้ว = *to understand now*
rúu	รู้	*to know*	+ lɛ́ɛu แล้ว = *to know already*
mii	มี	*to have*	+ lɛ́ɛu แล้ว = *to have already*
wái-tsai	ไว้ ใจ	*to trust*	+ lɛ́ɛu แล้ว = *to trust already*
rák	รัก	*to love*	+ lɛ́ɛu แล้ว = *to love now*
tsam-dâai	จำ ได้	*to remember*	+ lɛ́ɛu แล้ว = *to remember now*

rúu-sùk	รู้ สึก	*to feel*	+ lέεu แล้ว = *to feel now*
tʃɔ̂ɔp	ชอบ	*to like*	+ lέεu แล้ว = *to like now*
hěn-dûuai	เห็น ด้วย	*to agree*	+ lέεu แล้ว = *to agree now*
hěn	เห็น	*to see*	+ lέεu แล้ว = *to see now*
dâai-yin	ได้ ยิน	*to hear*	+ lέεu แล้ว = *to hear now*
dâai-klìn	ได้ กลิ่น	*to smell*	+ lέεu แล้ว = *to smell now*
tʃûua	เชื่อ	*to believe*	+ lέεu แล้ว = *to believe now*
sǒngsǎi	สงสัย	*to doubt*	+ lέεu แล้ว = *to doubt now*
klìiat	เกลียด	*to hate*	+ lέεu แล้ว = *to hate now*

- Sometimes, it is more natural to translate an adjective + **lέεu** แล้ว *already* as *now*.

13.3 Long term action verbs + lέεu แล้ว *already*

With long term action verbs the English tense often is the *present continuous tense* (action going on).

Examples:

> phǒm *tham-ngaan lέεu* ผม ทำ งาน แล้ว
> I *do-work already* – *I am already working.*

- In this sentence, long term action verb **tham-ngaan** ทำ งาน *to work* + **lέεu** แล้ว *already* express the state which has been reached; it is true now.

- In English, we express the same with the *present continuous tense* (I am working...)

> **2** tʃán *yùu* thîi tʃiiang-mài *lέεu* ฉัน อยู่ ที่ เชียงใหม่ แล้ว
> I *live* at Chiang Mai *already*
> *I am living in Chiang Mai now.*

- In this sentence, long term action verb **yùu** อยู่ *to live* + **lέεu** แล้ว *already* express the state which has been reached; it is true now.

- In English, we express the same with the *present continuous tense* (I am living...)

Longer term action verbs with some duration:

tham-ngaan	ทำ งาน	*to work*	+ lέεu แล้ว	= *to be already working*
yùu	อยู่	*to stay, to live*	+ lέεu แล้ว	= *to be living now*
riian	เรียน	*to study*	+ lέεu แล้ว	= *to be studying now*
nɔɔn	นอน	*to sleep*	+ lέεu แล้ว	= *to be already sleeping*
khàp	ขับ	*to drive*	+ lέεu แล้ว	= *to be driving*
kàsĭian	เกษียณ	*to retire*	+ lέεu แล้ว	= *to be already retired*

13.4 Short term action verbs + lέεu แล้ว *already*

With short term action verbs the English tense normally is the *present perfect tense* or *past simple tense* (the action completed).

Examples:

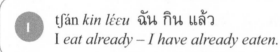

> ❶ tʃán *kin lέεu* ฉัน กิน แล้ว
> I *eat already* – I have already eaten.

- Here we have used the short term action verb **kin** กิน *to eat* + **lέεu** แล้ว *already*. The sentence expresses the state which has been reached; the action *has been completed*. The tense is understood from the context.

- In English, we express the same with the *present perfect tense* (I have eaten...)

> ❷ phŏm *bɔ̀ɔk* thəə *lέεu* ผม บอก เธอ แล้ว
> I *tell* she *already* – I have already told her.

- Here we have used the short term action verb **bɔ̀ɔk** บอก *to tell* + **lέɛu** แล้ว *already*. The sentence expresses the state which has been reached; the action *has been completed*. The tense is understood from the context.

- In English, we express the same here with the *present perfect tense* (I have told...)

Short term action verbs:

pai	ไป	*to go*	+ lέɛu แล้ว	= *have already gone*
maa	มา	*to come*	+ lέɛu แล้ว	= *have already come*
kin	กิน	*to eat*	+ lέɛu แล้ว	= *have already eaten*
sòng	ส่ง	*to send*	+ lέɛu แล้ว	= *have already sent*
tham	ทำ	*to do*	+ lέɛu แล้ว	= *have already done*
ɔ̀ɔk	ออก	*to leave*	+ lέɛu แล้ว	= *have already left*
thoo	โทร	*to call*	+ lέɛu แล้ว	= *have already called*
bɔ̀ɔk	บอก	*to tell*	+ lέɛu แล้ว	= *have already told*
lên	เล่น	*to play*	+ lέɛu แล้ว	= *have already played*
wîng	วิ่ง	*to run*	+ lέɛu แล้ว	= *have already run*
tʃái	ใช้	*to use*	+ lέɛu แล้ว	= *have already been used*
rɔ̂ɔm	เริ่ม	*to start*	+ lέɛu แล้ว	= *have already started*
tʃûuai	ช่วย	*to help*	+ lέɛu แล้ว	= *have already helped*

pháyaayaam พยายาม *to try* + lέɛu แล้ว = *have already tried*

◊

Chapter 14

Thai question words

Generally, Thai question words are placed at the end of the sentence. For different emphasis, some question words can also be placed at the beginning of the sentence.

14.1 Question words at the end of the sentence only

14.2 Question words at the end or at the beginning of the sentence

14.1 Question words at the end of the sentence only

Examples:

1. **mái** ไหม "question word"

> khrûːang níi dii *mái* เครื่อง นี้ ดี ไหม
> machine this good "*question*" – *Is this machine good?*

dii mái	ดี ไหม	*Is it good?*
tʃâi mái	ใช่ ไหม	*Right?*
dâai mái	ได้ ไหม	*Can I? Is it possible?*
pai mái	ไป ไหม	*Are you going?*
au mái	เอา ไหม	*Do you want?*

2. **rɯ̌ɯ** หรือ or?

> **2.1** khun tsà pai *rɯ̌ɯ-plàu* คุณ จะ ไป หรือ เปล่า
> you will go *or-not* – *Are you going or not?*

> **2.2** kin khâaw *rɯ̌ɯ-yang* กิน ข้าว หรือ ยัง
> eat rice *or-yet* – *Have you already eaten?*

rɯ̌ɯ-plàu	หรือ เปล่า	*or not?*
rɯ̌ɯ-yang	หรือ ยัง	*or not yet?*

3. **nǎi** ไหน which, where, what place?

> khun tsà pai *wan-nǎi* คุณ จะ ไป วัน ไหน
> you will go *day-which* – *Which day are you going?*

an-nǎi	อัน ไหน	*Which one?*
tîi-nǎi	ที่ ไหน	*Where? What place? Which place?*

| wan-năi | วัน ไหน | *Which day? What day?* |
| pai năi | ไป ไหน | *Where are you going?* |

4. **yang-ngai** ยังไง how?

> pai sànăam-bin *yang-ngai* ไป สนาม บิน ยังไง
> go field-fly *how – How to get to the airport?*

pai yang-ngai	ไป ยังไง	*How to get there?*
dâai yang-ngai	ได้ ยังไง	*How can I...?*
tham yang-ngai	ทำ ยังไง	*How to do it?*
tsàai yang-ngai	จ่าย ยังไง	*How to pay?*
tʃái yang-ngai	ใช้ ยังไง	*How to use it?*

5. **arai** อะไร what?

> khun yàak tham *arai* คุณ อยาก ทำ อะไร
> you want do *what – What do you want to do?*

| tʃûu arai | ชื่อ อะไร | *What is your name?* |
| an-níi arai | อัน นี้ อะไร | *What is this?* |

6. **ná** นะ and **lâ** ล่ะ?

> **6.1** *arai-ná* อะไร นะ
> *what-ná – What? Sorry? What did you say?*

● **ná** นะ cannot be directly translated into English.

> **6.2** phŏm sàbaai dii – léɛu *khun-lâ*
> ผม สบาย ดี – แล้ว คุณ ล่ะ
> I good – then *you-lâ*
> *I am good! – How about you? What about you?*

- Here **lâ** ละ is used when asking a counter question. It cannot be directly translated into English.

7. **tâu-rài** เท่าไร how much?

> **7.1** an-níi *tâu-rài* อัน นี้ เท่า ไร
> piece-this *equal-something – How much is this?*

> **7.2** rót khan níi raakhaa thâu-rai รถ คัน นี้ ราคา เท่าไร
> car vehicle this price *equal-something*
> *What is the price of this car?*

14.2 Question words *at the end* or at *the beginning* of the sentence

Examples:

1. **mûua-rai** เมื่อไร when?

> **1.1** *mûua-rai* khun tsà pai เมื่อไร คุณ จะ ไป
> *when* you will go – *When will you go?*

> **1.2** kháu maa *mûua-rai* เขา มา เมื่อไร
> he come *when* – *When did he come?*

2. **krai** ใคร who, whom, whose?

> **2.1** *khrai* tsà pai ใคร จะ ไป
> *who* will go – *Who is going?*

> **2.2** khun yùu kàp *khrai* คุณ อยู่ กับ ใคร
> you stay with *who* – *With whom are you staying?*

2.3 an-níi kɔ̌ɔng *khrai* อัน นี้ ของ ใคร
piece-this of *who – Whose is this?*

3. thammai ทำไม why?

3.1 kháu tsà pai *thammai* เขา จะ ไป ทำไม
he will go *why – Why is he going?*

3.2 *thammai* khun mâi maa ทำ ไม คุณ ไม่ มา
why you no come – *Why didn't you come?*

4. kìi กี่ how many?

4.1 maa *kìi* khon มา กี่ คน
come *how-many* person – *How many people came?*

4.2 *kìi* khon maa กี่ คน มา
how-many person come – *How many people came?*

4.3 tsà tsəə *kìi* moong จะ เจอ กี่ โมง
will meet *how-many* hour
What time are we going to meet?

- The usage of **kìi** กี่ *how many* is somewhat special. It is normally placed before a classifier; here it isplaced before **khon** คน *person* and **moong** โมง *hour*. It can also be placed between the verb and the classifier. See the first sentence 4.1.

◊

Chapter 15

Prepositions

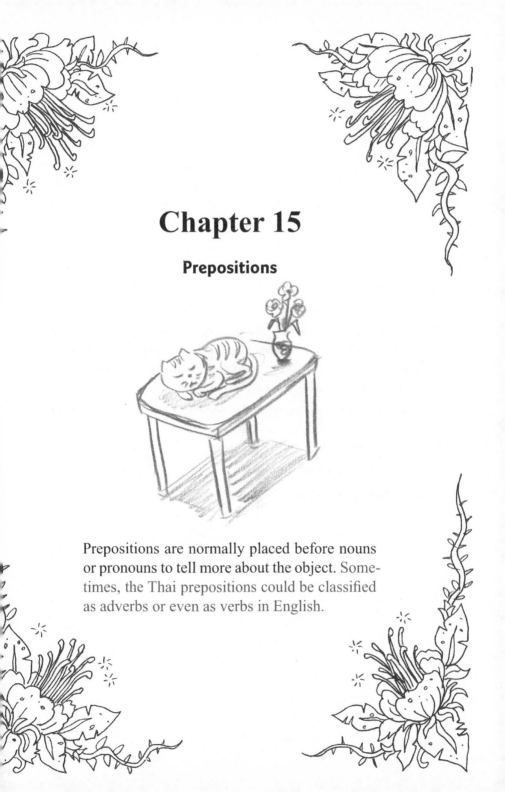

Prepositions are normally placed before nouns or pronouns to tell more about the object. Sometimes, the Thai prepositions could be classified as adverbs or even as verbs in English.

In Thai, we are not very much concerned with classifications of different words such as adjectives, verbs, adverbs, prepositions, etc. They are just words to make the meaning clear. However, the English categories give us a chance to identify many important words, which we need to express ourselves in different situations.

15.1   Simple prepositions

15.2   Prepositions of location

15.3   Time prepositions

15.1 Simple prepositions

Examples:

> **1**   an-níi *sǎmràp* khun   อัน นี้ สำหรับ คุณ
> piece-this *for* you – *This is for you.*

- Here we have placed the preposition **sǎmràp** สำหรับ *for* before the pronoun **khun** คุณ *you.*

> **2**   an-níi *hâi* khun   อัน นี้ ให้ คุณ
> piece-this *for* you – *This is for you.*

- We could also use the verb **hâi** ให้ *to give* instead of **sǎmràp** สำหรับ *for*; the translation into English would be the same, *for.*

- **hâi** ให้ *to give, for* is more familiar style and is commonly used in speaking.

tsàak	จาก	*from*
sǎmràp	สำหรับ	*for*
hâi	ให้	*for, to give*
phûɯa	เพื่อ	*for, in order to*
tʃên	เช่น	*for example, as, like*
khɔ̌ɔng	ของ	*of*
kìiau-kàp	เกี่ยว กับ	*about*
kàp	กับ	*with*
phàan, ləəi	ผ่าน, เลย	*past*
thâu-nán	เท่า นั้น	*only*
kùap	เกือบ	*almost*
dooi	โดย	*by*
dûuai	ด้วย	*by, with*
taam	ตาม	*according to*

15.2 Prepositions of location

One important function of prepositions of location is to indicate the position of the object.

yùu *bon* tó อยู่ บน โต๊ะ
stay *on* table – *It is on the table.*

- Here we have placed the preposition **bon** บน *on* before the noun **tó** โต๊ะ *table.*

thîi	ที่	*at, in, to*
nai	ใน	*in*
nɔ̂ɔk	นอก	*out*
bon	บน	*on*
tâi	ใต้	*under*
lăng	หลัง	*after, behind*
ráwàang	ระหว่าง	*between*
klâi	ใกล้	*near*
klai	ไกล	*far*
kɔ̀ɔn	ก่อน	*before* (a place or time)
trong	ตรง	*straight*
trong-níi	ตรง นี้	*over here, right here*
trong-nán	ตรง นั้น	*over there, right there*
trong-khâam	ตรง ข้าม	*opposite, across*
trong-nâa	ตรง หน้า	*right in front of...*
thɛ̆ɛu	แถว	*around*
thɛ̆ɛu-níi	แถว นี้	*around here*
thɛ̆ɛu-thɛ̆ɛu	แถวๆ	*around here somewhere*
thaang	ทาง	*away, path*

thaang-bòk	ทาง บก	*by land*
thaang-náam	ทาง น้ำ	*by sea, by boat*
thaang-aakàat	ทาง อากาศ	*by air*
thaang-rót-yon	ทาง รถ ยนต์	*by car, by road*
thaang-khrûuang-bin	ทาง เครื่อง บิน	*by air*
khâang	ข้าง	*next to, alongside*
khâang-khâang	ข้างๆ	*next to, near*
khâang-lâang	ข้าง ล่าง	*downstairs*
khâang-bon	ข้าง บน	*upstairs*
phaai	ภาย	*side, part*
phaai-nai	ภาย ใน	*inside*
phaai-nɔ̂ɔk	ภาย นอก	*outside*
phaai-tâi	ภาย ใต้	*under*

15.3 Time prepositions

Time prepositions are used to tell more about the specific time when something happens.

Example:

> tsɔɔ kan *tɔɔn-bàai* เจอ กัน ตอน บ่าย
> meet with *during-afternoon – Let's meet in the afternoon.*

- Here we have placed the preposition **tɔɔn** ตอน *at, during* before the word **bàai** บ่าย *afternoon.*

tɔɔn	ตอน	*during, at*
tɔɔn-níi	ตอน นี้	*now*
tɔɔn-nán	ตอน นั้น	*then, by then*
tɔɔn-thîi	ตอน ที่	*when, as*
tɔɔn-tʃáu	ตอน เช้า	*in the morning*

tɔɔn-bàai	ตอน บ่าย	*early afternoon*
tɔɔn-yen	ตอน เย็น	*late afternoon*
tɔɔn-khâm	ตอน ค่ำ	*in the evening*
níi	นี้	*this*
dǐiau-níi	เดี๋ยว นี้	*now, instantly*
khànà-níi	ขณะ นี้	*at this moment*
khraau-níi	คราว นี้	*this occasion, now*
khráng-níi	ครั้ง นี้	*this time, now*
pàt-tsùban-níi	ปัจจุบัน นี้	*nowadays*
thúk-wan-níi	ทุก วัน นี้	*nowadays, at present*
lǎng	หลัง	*after, later*
lǎng-tsàak	หลัง จาก	*after*
thii-lǎng	ที หลัง	*afterwards*
mûɯa	เมื่อ	*when, at (*often refers to the past)
mûɯa-kɔ̀ɔn	เมื่อ ก่อน	*previously*
mûɯa-waan	เมื่อวาน	*yesterday*
mûɯa-khɯɯn	เมื่อ คืน	*last night*
mûɯa-kîi	เมื่อ กี้	*a moment ago*
mûɯa-tʃáu-níi	เมื่อ เช้า นี้	*this morning* (past)
thîi-lɛ́ɛu	ที่ แล้ว	*time in the past*
dɯɯan thîi-lɛ́ɛu	เดือน ที่ แล้ว	*last month*
khráng thîi-lɛ́ɛu	ครั้ง ที่ แล้ว	*last time*
tʃâat thîi-lɛ́ɛu	ชาติ ที่ แล้ว	*previous life*
nâa	หน้า	*front, future*
khráng-nâa	ครั้ง หน้า	*next time*
dɯɯan-nâa	เดือน หน้า	*next month*
pii-nâa	ปี หน้า	*next year*

khâang-nâa	ข้าง หน้า	*in front of, future* (time and place)
wan-khâang-nâa	วัน ข้าง หน้า	*following days*
phaai-nâa	ภาย หน้า	*future*
nai-phaai-nâa	ใน ภาย หน้า	*following days*
phaai-nai	ภาย ใน	*within*
nai-weelaa	ใน เวลา	*at, during*
ráwàang	ระหว่าง	*during, meantime* (time and place)
tson, tson-thŭng	จน, จน ถึง	*until*
tâng-tɛ̀ɛ	ตั้ง แต่	*since*

Chapter 16

Conjunction words

Conjunction words are used to connect
words, phrases and sentences.

Some commonly used conjunction words

Examples:

> tʃán súu sûua-yûut *kàp* kràpăo
> ฉัน ซื้อ เสื้อ ยืด กับ กระเป๋า
> I puy shirt- stretch *with* bag
> *I bought a T-shirt and a bag.*

- Here **kàp** กับ *and, with* connects two nouns. We could have used
  lɛ́ และ *and* or **lɛ́ɛu-kɔ̂ɔ** แล้ว ก็ *and, and then*. The meaning would
  have been the same.

lɛ́	และ	*and*
kàp	กับ	*and, with*
lɛ́ɛu	แล้ว	*then, after that*
lɛ́ɛu-kɔ̂ɔ	แล้ว ก็	*and, and then*
lɛ́ɛu-yang	แล้ว ยัง	*and in addition, besides*
lɛ́ɛu-thǔng	แล้ว ถึง	*and when done, after finishing*
tɛ̀ɛ	แต่	*but*

> phǒm yàak pai *tɛ̀ɛ-wâa* mâi mii weelaa
> ผม อยาก ไป แต่ ว่า ไม่ มี เวลา
> I want go *but-that* no have time
> *I want to go, but I don't have time.*

- Here **tɛ̀ɛ-wâa** แต่ ว่า *but* connects two independent clauses.

wâa	ว่า	*that*
tɛ̀ɛ-wâa	แต่ ว่า	*but*
phrɔ́	เพราะ	*because*
phrɔ́-wâa	เพราะ ว่า	*because*
rǔu	หรือ	*or*

thâa	ถ้า	*if*
mûua	เมื่อ	*when (past)*
weelaa	เวลา	*when*
tɔɔn-thîi	ตอน ที่	*while, when, as*
kɔ̀ɔn-thîi	ก่อน ที่	*before*
lăng-tsàak-thîi	หลัง จาก ที่	*after*
kɔ̂ɔ-ləəi	ก็ เลย	*therefore, so, as a result*

phŏm maa thîi-nîi *phûua* long-thábiian
ผม มา ที่ นี่ เพื่อ ลง ทะเบียน
I come place-this *for* down-register
I came here to register.

- Here **phûua** เพื่อ *in order to, for* connects two clauses.

dang-nán	ดัง นั้น	*therefore, in consequence* (formal)
phûua	เพื่อ	*in order to, for*
nɔ̂ɔk-tsàak	นอก จาก	*except, apart from, besides*
tson-kwàa	จน กว่า	*until, by the time*
yàang	อย่าง	*as*
tʃên	เช่น	*as*

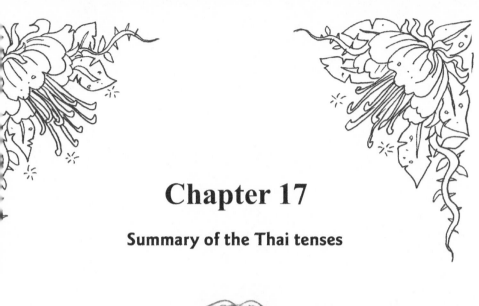

Chapter 17

Summary of the Thai tenses

Tenses in Thai can be expressed in many different ways. For more information, you may also wish to review the previous Chapters 12, 13 and 15.

17.1 Basic sentence

In many cases, the tense in Thai is understood from the context; hence, there is not any need for additional indicators. The basic sentence is a sentence which does not have any time word, tense marker or any other indicator which points out the tense. Yet, the basic sentence in Thai can be translated into English as the present, past or future tense.

Example:

> phŏm tʃɔ̂ɔp kháu ผม ชอบ เขา
> I like she – *I like her.*

- Here the English tense is the present simple tense.

17.2 Talking about *when*

The *time words* refer to a definite time or tense in Thai. They answer the question *when*. The tense in Thai can be made more clear with the *time words* such as **tɔɔn-níi** ตอน นี้ *now, this moment*, **mûua-waan** เมื่อวาน *yesterday* and **phrûng-níi** พรุ่งนี้ *tomorrow*. The time words are very important tools to express the correct tense in Thai.

Example:

> *mûua-waan* tʃán pai thîiau เมื่อวาน ฉัน ไป เที่ยว
> *yesterday* I go out – *Yesterday, I went out.*

- Here the English tense is the past simple tense.
- The past time word **mûua-waan** เมื่อวาน *yesterday* is placed at the beginning of the sentence. For different emphasis, we could place it at the end of the sentence.

Present time words:

tɔɔn-níi	ตอน นี้	*now, this moment*
dǐiau-níi	เดี๋ยว นี้	*now, instantly, nowadays*
pàt-tsùban	ปัจจุบัน	*nowadays*

Past time words:

mûua-waan	เมื่อวาน	*yesterday*
pii thîi-lέεu	ปี ที่ แล้ว	*a year ago*
mûua-kɔ̀ɔn	เมื่อ ก่อน	*earlier, before*

Future time words:

phrûng-níi	พรุ่ง นี้	*tomorrow*
pii-nâa	ปี หน้า	*next year*
ìik-sǎam-wan	อีก สาม วัน	*in three days*

17.3 Talking about *how often*

The *time words of frequency* tell *how often* something happens. The time words of frequency are concerned with *how often* the action takes place in the *present time*, did take place in the *past*, or will take place in the *future*.

Example:

> phǒm maa thîi-níi *thúk-wan* ผม มา ที่ นี่ ทุก วัน
> I come place-this *every-day* – *I come here everyday.*

- Here the English tense is the present simple tense.
- The time word **thúk-wan** ทุก วัน *every day* is placed at the end of the sentence. For different emphasis, we could place it at the beginning of the sentence.

The common time words of frequency:

bɔ̀i	บ่อย	*often*
pòkkàtì	ปกติ	*usually*
sàmɔ̌ɔ	เสมอ	*always*
thúk-wan	ทุก วัน	*every day*
pràtsam	ประจำ	*regularly*

17.4 Talking about the time indicators

The *time indicators* such as **léɛu** แล้ว *already, state* or *condition reached, attained* and **yùu** อยู่ *state* or *condition exists* are used as *indicators* to place emphasis on the relevant action, state or condition in relation to time (certain tense) in Thai. **léɛu** แล้ว can be used in the present, past or future time sentences while **yùu** อยู่ is commonly used for actions which happen in the present time, *now* or *nowadays*.

Examples:

> **1** fǒn-tòk *léɛu* ฝน ตก แล้ว
> rain-fall *already* – *It is already raining.*

> **2** fǒn-tòk *yùu* ฝน ตก แล้ว
> rain-fall *be* – *It is raining.*

- Here the English tense is the present continuous tense.

- **léɛu** แล้ว *already* expresses the fact that the rain has started while **yùu** อยู่ *state exists* expresses the fact that it has been raining for a while or even for a longer time.

17.5 Talking about the present tense markers

kamlang กำลัง and **yùu** อยู่ are used for actions which are happening at the time of speaking.

kamlang กำลัง *action in progress* and **yùu** อยู่ *state exists* are used grammatically differently. Strictly speaking, **yùu** อยู่ *state exists* is not a tense marker. However, the meaning is very similar to **kamlang** กำลัง *action in progress*.

Therefore, we review it also with the tense marker **kamlang** กำลัง. The present tense marker **kamlang** กำลัง is placed *before the action verb* while **yùu** อยู่ usually comes *at the end of the sentence*.

Example:

> tʃán *kamlang* tham aahǎan *yùu* ฉัน กำลัง ทำ อาหาร อยู่
> I *kamlang* do food *be – I am making food.*

- Here the English tense is the present continuous tense.

- The helping verb **kamlang** กำลัง *action in progress* is placed before the main verb **tham** ทำ *to do,* and the time indicator **yùu** อยู่ *state exist* is placed at the end of the sentence.

17.6 Talking about the past time tense markers

In Thai, there are several ways to indicate that the action has taken place in the past. By using the past tense markers **khɔɔi** เคย *once, used to* or **phɯ̂ng** เพิ่ง *just* makes it clear that the action has happened in the past. They are always placed *before the action verb*.

Examples:

> **1** khun *khɔɔi* pai pràthêet wîiatnaam mái
> คุณ เคย ไป ประเทศ เวียดนาม ไหม
> you *once* go country Vietnam "question"
> *Have you ever been to Vietnam?*

> **2** tʃán *phɯ̂ng* tham ฉัน เพิ่ง ทำ
> I *just* do – *I have just done it.*

- Here the English tense is the present perfect tense.

- The helping verbs **khɔɔi** เคย *once* and **phɯ̂ng** เพิ่ง *just* are placed before the main verbs **pai** ไป *to go* and **tham** ทำ *to do* respectively.

17.7 Talking about the future tense marker

The future tense marker **tsà** จะ *will* is often used when talking about future plans, intentions and promises. Thai people use **tsà** จะ in a hypothetical manner to talk about possible future actions. It is used in a similar way as the English helping verb *will*. **tsà** จะ is always placed *before the action verb*.

Example:

> phŏm *tsà* súu rót mài ผม จะ ซื้อ รถ ใหม่
> I *will* buy car new – *I will buy a new car.*

- Here the English tense is the future simple tense.

- The helping verb **tsà** จะ *will* is placed before the main verb **súu** ซื้อ *to buy.*

17.8 Talking about the duration of time and point of time

1.   The Thai language often uses *direction verbs* such as **maa** มา *to come* and **pai** ไป *to go* in order to express the correct time frame. They are placed *before the duration of time*. **dâai** ได้ can be used alone or with **maa** มา to perform the same function. So, we have the following four ways to choose from: **dâai** ได้, **maa** มา, **maa-dâai** มา ได้, **pai** ไป.

When these helping verbs are placed before the duration of time, they are usually translated into English as *for: for so many months, days, hours, minutes, etc.*

Example:

> kháu khàp rót-théksîi *maa* săam pii lέεu
> เขา ขับ รถ แท็กซี่ มา สาม ปี แล้ว
> he drive car-taxi long *come* three year already
> *He has been driving a taxi for three years.*

- Here the English tense is the present perfect continuous tense.

- The helping verb **maa** มา *to come* is placed before the duration of time **săam pii** สาม ปี *three years.*

It depends much on the personal style and feeling whether we use **dâai** ได้, **maa** มา, **maa-dâai** มา ได้ or **pai** ไป before the duration of time in the sentence.

The emphasis is as follows:

dâai	ได้	*for, to get* (feeling of getting it)
maa	มา	*for, to come* (feeling of having it)
maa-dâai	มา ได้	*for, come-get* (feeling of having and getting it)
pai	ไป	*for, to go* (feeling of indifference or losing it)

2. Point of time (since) is expressed in the similar ways as in English.

The preposition **tâng-tὲὲ** ตั้ง แต่ *since* is placed before the point of time. It expresses the point of time when the action was started.

Example:

> kháu khàp rót-théksîi *tâng-tὲὲ* pii thîi-lέεu
> เขา ขับ รถ แท็กซี่ ตั้ง แต่ ปี ที่ แล้ว
> he drive car-taxi long *set-since* year that-already
> *He has been driving a taxi since last year.*

- Here the English tense is the present perfect continuous tense.

- The preposition **tâng-tὲὲ** ตั้ง แต่ *since* is placed before the point of time **pii thîi-lέεu** ปี ที่ แล้ว *last year.*

3. There are a few books about how to use Thai tenses:

a) Dhyan Manik: *Learning Thai Tenses with dâai* ได้ *Book II*

b) David Smyth: *Thai – An Essential Grammar*

c) Higbie & Thinsan: *Thai Reference Grammar – The Structure of Spoken Thai*

d) Dhyan Manik: Learning *Thai and Thai Tenses with lέεu* แล้ว (coming out late 2020)

◊

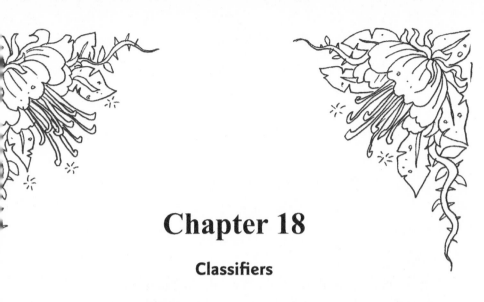

Chapter 18

Classifiers

Thai classifiers are also called count words or measure words. It is impossible to speak correct Thai if you don't have some basic knowledge about classifiers.

Classifiers are used in Thai whenever the main verb is qualified by a number (three books), adverb (some books, many books) or by a pronoun (this book, that book). There are several hundred classifiers in Thai. We study here the most common ones.

When a classifier is used rarely, sometimes even native speakers would have difficulty to remember the correct classifier.

18.1   Similar classifiers (Thai vs English)

18.2   A classifier as the main noun

18.3   Classifiers with specific meaning

18.4   Classifiers used for differnt types of nouns

18.1 Similar classifiers (Thai vs English)

In English, we also use classifiers such as days, years, bottles, glasses, buckets, bags, etc. Some common Thai classifiers are used in the similar way.

Examples:

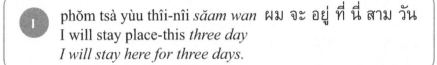

> **①** phǒm tsà yùu thîi-nîi *sǎam wan* ผม จะ อยู่ ที่ นี่ สาม วัน
> I will stay place-this *three day*
> *I will stay here for three days.*

- In Thai, the count number is always placed before the classifier. Here the number **sǎam** สาม *three* is placed before the classifier **wan** วัน *day*. The structure is similar in English.

> **②** mii *nùng rɔ́ɔi khon* nai roong-riian
> มี หนึ่ง ร้อย คน ใน โรง เรียน
> have *one hundred person* in building-study
> *There are one hundred people in the school.*

- This structure is grammatically similar in Thai and in English. **khon** คน *person* is a classifier.

- **khon** คน *person, people* as a classifier is also used in English. For example **tsèt khon** เจ็ด คน is translated into English as *seven people*. The difference is that in Thai we always need to use the classifier **khon** คน when we are referring to people.

> **③** mii *nák-riian nùng rɔ́ɔi khon* nai roong-riian
> มี นัก เรียน หนึ่ง ร้อย คน ใน โรง เรียน
> have *nák-study one hundred person* in building-study
> *There are one hundred students in the school.*

- In English, we can place the number before the main noun and say *one hundred students*. In Thai, the number is always placed before a classifier; hence, we must say *student one hundred persons*.

- In Thai, it would be grammatically incorrect to say **nùng rɔ́ɔi nák-riian** หนึ่ง ร้อย นัก เรียน *one hundred students*. Thais would never make that type of mistake. It would sound very weird to the Thai ear.

wan	วัน	*day*
aathít	อาทิตย์	*week*
dɯɯan	เดือน	*month*
pii	ปี	*year*
khon	คน	*person, people*
thûuai	ถ้วย	*cup, anything served in cups*
kɛ̂ɛu	แก้ว	*glass, anything served in glasses*
tsaan	จาน	*plate, anything served in plates*
khùuat	ขวด	*bottle, anything served in bottles*
khráng	ครั้ง	*times*
kìloo	กิโล	*kilogram*
méet	เมตร	*meter*
kìloo-méet	กิโล เมตร	*kilometer*
bàat	บาท	*bath*
yuuroo	ยูโร	*euro*
dɔɔnlâa	ดอลลาร์	*dollar*
pɔɔn	ปอนด์	*pound*
yeen	เยน	*yen*

18.2 A classifier as the main noun

With some words, the classifier is the same as the main noun. Formally, a classifier is then repeated. However, in informal speech the classifier is commonly spoken only once.

Examples:

 bâan tʃán mii *hɔ̂ng lǎai hɔ̂ng* บ้าน ฉัน มี ห้อง หลาย ห้อง
home I have *room many room*
My home has many rooms.

- In this sentence, the main noun is also a classifier, **hɔ̂ng** ห้อง *room.*

So, in casual speech, the above sentence can be written like this:

 bâan tʃán mii *lǎai hɔ̂ng* บ้าน ฉัน มี หลาย ห้อง
home I have *many room* – *My home has many rooms.*

- The main noun is often dropped. Hence, **hɔ̂ng** ห้อง *room* is used only once. That is perhaps because it sounds a bit too overwhelming to say the same word twice.

hɔ̂ng	ห้อง	*rooms*
roong-rian	โรง เรียน	*schools*
roong-rɛɛm	โรง แรม	*hotels*
khon	คน	*person, people*
kham	คำ	*words*
klɔ̀ɔng	กล่อง	*boxes*
wíthii	วิธี	*ways, methods*
rûup	รูป	*pictures*
phleeng	เพลง	*songs*
wát	วัด	*temple*

18.3 Classifiers with specific meaning

Example:

> tʃán tʃɔ̂ɔp aahǎan *thúk-yàang* ฉัน ชอบ อาหาร ทุก อย่าง
> I like food *all-kind – I like all kinds of food.*

- In this sentence, the main noun is **aahǎan** อาหาร *food*. In Thai, the number or quantifier is always placed before a classifier. Here **thúk** ทุก *all* is placed before the classifier **yàang** อย่าง *kinds.*

thîi	ที่	*places, seats*
hɛ̀ɛng	แห่ง	*places, locations*
hɔ̀ɔ	ห่อ	*things wrapped in bundles or packages*
phɯ̌ɯn	ผืน	*pieces of cloth, blanket, scarf...*
tʃín	ชิ้น	*pieces of anything, pieces of bread, fruits...*
fɔɔng	ฟอง	*eggs*
dɔ̀ɔk	ดอก	*flowers*
tʃɔ̂ɔ	ช่อ	*bouquets of flowers, clusters...*
phǒn	ผล	*for all kinds of fruit*
khànàat	ขนาด	*sizes and dimensions*
tʃánít	ชนิด	*types, kinds, sorts of things*
yàang	อย่าง	*way, sorts, types, kinds*

18.4 Classifiers used for differnt types of nouns

These kinds of classifiers are a bit challenging since they are used for many different nouns, and sometimes there does not seem to be any particular reason why a classifier is used for the particular noun.

Example:

> tʃán súɯ *năng-sŭɯ* sɔ̌ɔng *lêm* lɛ́ɛu-kɔ̂ɔ *thiian* sìp *lêm*
>
> ฉัน ซื้อ หนังสือ สอง เล่ม แล้ว ก็ เทียน สิบ เล่ม
>
> I buy *book* two *copy* then-also *candle* ten *piece*
>
> *I bought two books and ten candles.*

- Here we have used the classifier **lêm** เล่ม for **năng-súɯ** หนังสือ *book* and for **thiian** เทียน *candle*. **lêm** เล่ม is also commonly used for *knives* and some sharp objects such as *rods* and *scissors*.

an	อัน	used for many small objects such as *toothpicks, pieces of cakes, ashtrays, etc.*
bai	ใบ	*bags, glasses, cups, fruits, eggs, plates, sheets of paper, tickets*
lûuk	ลูก	*round objects, fruits, balls, etc.*
mét	เม็ด	*gems, pills, tablets, seeds, buttons, etc.*
khrûɯang	เครื่อง	*machines, refrigerators, computers, electrical devises, etc.*
khan	คัน	*cars, spoons, forks, umbrellas, etc.*
khàbuuan	ขบวน	*trains, convoys, marching soldiers, etc.*
lam	ลำ	*long objects, airplains, boats, ships, sugar cane, bamboo, etc.*
lêm	เล่ม	*books, knives, candles, axes, pins, needles*
tuua	ตัว	*animals, clothes, chairs, tables, letters (alphabets), etc.*
tʃút	ชุด	*suits, sets of furniture, series of things, team of players*
khûu	คู่	*pairs of various things such as shoes, pairs of animals*
tʃàbàp	ฉบับ	*documents, letters, papers with printings and writings on them*

muuan	มวน	*cigarettes*
tôn	ต้น	*trees, plants, pillars, columns, posts*
sên	เส้น	*ropes, lines, threads, strands of hair, strings, cables, roads, long things, belts, bracelets, necklets*
sǎai	สาย	*ropes, strings, roads, rivers*
thɛ̌ɛu	แถว	*columns, rows, lines, strings*
phɛ̀ɛn	แผ่น	*flat and thin objects, sheets of paper, slices of bread, CD's*
sɔɔng	ซอง	*envelopes, packets of cigarettes*
duuang	ดวง	*stars, lights, postage stamps*
kɔ̂ɔn	ก้อน	*cubes of sugar, lumps, chunks, pieces of charcoal, bricks, rocks, clouds*

Chapter 19

Prefixes

Prefixes are important grammar components in Thai. It is impossible to speak correct Thai if you don't have some basic knowledge about prefixes.

19.1   Commonly used general prefixes

19.1.1 khwaam ความ *matter* prefix turns verbs or adjectives into abstract nouns

19.1.2 kaan การ *task* prefix normally turns verbs into nouns (-ing)

19.1.3 khîi ขี้ prefix before adjectives often refers to some negative quality

19.1.4 nâa น่า *worthy of* prefix indicates a certain condition (often in English *-ing*)

19.1.5 náam น้ำ *water, liquids* can be used as a prefix or as a suffix. When used as a prefix náam น้ำ is normally pronounced short as nám น้ำ.

19.1.6 kham คำ means *word* or *words* and is used as a prefix to make nouns out of verbs that refer to something that has been written or said

19.1.7 khâa ค่า is a noun and means *price*. It is used as a prefix to make compound words that refer to prices, amounts of money and charges for different things

19.1.8 khɔ̂ɔ ข้อ is used as a prefix to make compound words, normally nouns, which can refer to text, information, point, clause in the contract, etc.

19.1 Commonly used general prefixes

Example:

1. khwaam   ความ   *matter*
2. kaan   การ   *task*
3. khîi   ขี้   indicates a negative quality before adjectives
4. nâa   น่า   *worthy of*
5. náam   น้ำ   *water, liquids*
6. kham   คำ   *word, words*
7. khâa   ค่า   *price, prices*
8. khɔ̂ɔ   ข้อ   *point, text*

19.1.1 khwaam ความ *matter* prefix turns verbs or adjectives into abstract nouns

Example:

> khruu tông mii *khwaam-rúu* ครู ต้อง มี ความ รู้
> teacher must have *matter-know*
> *A teacher must have knowledge.*

- Here the prefix **kwaam** ความ *matter* is placed before the verb **rúu** รู้ *to know*. **khwaam-rúu** ความ รู้ becomes a noun, *knowledge*.

khwaam-tsing	ความ จริง	*truth*
khwaam-khít	ความ คิด	*idea*
khwaam-sùk	ความ สุข	*happiness*
khwaam-rúu	ความ รู้	*knowledge*
khwaam-rák	ความ รัก	*love*
khwaam-rɔ́ɔn	ความ ร้อน	*heat, hotness*
khwaam-reu	ความ เร็ว	*speed, quickness*

19.1.2 kaan การ *task* prefix normally turns verbs into nouns (-ing)

Example:

> *kaan-dəən* dii การ เดิน ดี
> *task-walk* good – *Walking is good.*

- Here the prefix **kaan** การ *task* is placed before the verb **dəən** เดิน *to walk*. **kaan-dəən** การ เดิน becomes a noun, *walking*.

kaan-àan	การ อ่าน	*reading*
kaan-bin	การ บิน	*flying*
kaan-fùk	การ ฝึก	*practising*
kaan-dəən	การ เดิน	*walking*
kaan-duu	การ ดู	*looking*
kaan-lên	การ เล่น	*playing*
kaan-khâu	การ เข้า	*entry, entering*
kaan-hâi	การ ให้	*giving*
kaan-dâai-ráp	การ ได้ รับ	*receiving*

19.1.3 khîi ขี้ prefix before adjectives often refers to some negative quality

Example:

> bang khon *khîi-luum* mâak-mâak บาง คน ขี้ ลืม มากๆ
> some person *khîi-forget* very-very
> *Some people are really forgetful.*

- Here we have placed the prefix **khîi** ขี้ before the verb **luum** ลืม *to forget*. **khîi-luum** ขี้ ลืม becomes an adjective, *to be forgetful*.

khîi-kìiat	ขี้ เกียจ	*to be lazy*
khîi-aai	ขี้ อาย	*to be shy*

khîi-luum	ขี้ ลืม	*to be forgetful*
khîi nǐiau	ขี้ เหนียว	*to be stingy*
khîi hǔng	ขี้ หึง	*to be jealous*
khîi-bòn	ขี้ บ่น	*to be complaining*
khîi-mau	ขี้ เมา	*to be an alcoholic*
khîi-phέε	ขี้ แพ้	*to be a loser*

19.1.4 nâa น่า *worthy of* prefix indicates a certain condition (often in English *-ing*)

Example:

> kháu *nâa-rák* tsang เขา น่า รัก จัง
> she *nâa-love* very – *She is very cute.*

- Here **nâa** น่า *worthy of* is placed before the verb **rák** รัก *to love*. The meaning becomes *cute, lovely.*

nâa-rák	น่า รัก	*to be cute, pretty*
nâa-mɔɔng	น่า มอง	*to be charming*
nâa-sǒn-tsai	น่า สน ใจ	*to be interesting*
nâa-yùu	น่า อยู่	*to be pleasant, liveable*
nâa-arɔ̀i	น่า อร่อย	*to be delicious*
nâa-khǎn	น่า ขัน	*to be funny, amusing*
nâa-kluua	น่า กลัว	*to be frightening*
nâa-bùua	น่า เบื่อ	*to be boring*

19.1.5 náam น้ำ *water, liquids* **can be used as a prefix or as a suffix. When used as a prefix náam** น้ำ **is normally pronounced short as nám** น้ำ

Example:

> *nám-nàk* khun thâu-rai น้ำ หนัก คุณ เท่าไร
> *water-heavy* you equal-what – *How much is your weigth?*

- Here we have placed the prefix **náam** น้ำ *water* before the adjective **nàk** หนัก *to be heavy.* **nám-nàk** น้ำ หนัก becomes a noun, *weight.*

Prefix:

nám-khěng	น้ำ แข็ง	*ice*
nám-man	น้ำ มัน	*oil*
nám-taa	น้ำ ตา	*tears*
nám-taan	น้ำ ตาล	*sugar, brown*
nám-tòk	น้ำ ตก	*waterfall*
nám-thûuam	น้ำ ท่วม	*flood*
nám-nàk	น้ำ หนัก	*weight*

Suffix:

hɔ̂ng-náam	ห้อง น้ำ	*bathroom, toilet*
mɛ̂ɛ-náam	แม่ น้ำ	*river*
àap-náam	อาบ น้ำ	*to take a shower*
lên-náam	เล่น น้ำ	*to play in the water, to swim*
wâai-náam	ว่าย น้ำ	*to swim*
dam-náam	ดำ น้ำ	*to dive*
rádàp-náam	ระดับ น้ำ	*water level*

19.1.6 kham คำ means *word* or *words* and is used as a prefix to make nouns out of verbs that refer to something that has been written or said

Example:

rau dâai-ráp *kham-tʃɔɔn* lɛ́ɛu เรา ได้ รับ คำ เชิญ แล้ว
we get-receive *word-invite* already
We have aready received an invitation.

- Here we have placed the prefix **kham** คำ *word* before the verb **tʃɔɔn** เชิญ *to invite*. **kham-tʃɔɔn** คำ เชิญ becomes a noun, *invitation*.

kham-thǎam	คำ ถาม	*question, inquiry*
kham-tɔ̀ɔp	คำ ตอบ	*answer, reply*
kham-nɛ́-nam	คำ แนะ นำ	*advice, suggestion*
kham-plɛɛ	คำ แปล	*translation*
kham-sǎnyaa	คำ สัญญา	*promise*
kham-nam	คำ นำ	*introduction, preface*
kham-tʃɔɔn	คำ เชิญ	*invitation*
kham-athíbaai	คำ อธิบาย	*explanation*

19.1.7 khâa ค่า is a noun and means *price*. It is used as a prefix to make compound words that refer to prices, amounts of money and charges for different things

Example:

khâa-riian mâi phɛɛŋ ค่า เรียน ไม่ แพง
price-study no expensive – *The school fee is not expensive.*

- Here we have placed the prefix **khâa** ค่า *price* before the verb **riian** เรียน *to study*. **khâa-riian** ค่า เรียน becomes a noun, *school fee*.

khâa-thoorásàp	ค่า โทรศัพท์	*telephone bill*
khâa-dəən-thaang	ค่า เดิน ทาง	*travel cost*
khâa-riian	ค่า เรียน	*school fee*
khâa-tǔua	ค่า ตั๋ว	*ticket fee, fare*
khâa-phaasǐi	ค่า ภาษี	*tax, duty*
khâa-fai	ค่า ไฟ	*electricity bill*
khâa-tʃâu	ค่า เช่า	*rental fee*
khâa-bɔɔríkaan	ค่า บริการ	*service charge, service fees*

19.1.8 khɔ̂ɔ ข้อ is used as a prefix to make compound words, normally nouns, which can refer to text, information, point, clause in the contract, etc.

Example:

> *khɔ̂ɔ-sànə̌ə* khun dii ข้อ เสนอ คุณ ดี
> *item-offe*r you good – *Your proposal was good.*

- Here we have placed the prefix **khɔ̂ɔ** ข้อ *item, point* before the verb **sànə̌ə** เสนอ *to offer, to propose.* **khɔ̂ɔ-sànə̌ə** ข้อ เสนอ becomes a noun, *offer, proposal.*

khɔ̂ɔ-dii	ข้อ ดี	*merit, good point*
khɔ̂ɔ-muun	ข้อ มูล	*data, information*
khɔ̂ɔ-khwaam	ข้อ ความ	*message, statement, SMS*
khɔ̂ɔ-sɔ̌ɔp	ข้อ สอบ	*examination, test*
khɔ̂ɔ-sànə̌ə	ข้อ เสนอ	*proposal, offer*
khɔ̂ɔ-sǎnyaa	ข้อ สัญญา	*items in the contract*
khɔ̂ɔ-mɯɯ	ข้อ มือ	*wrist*

19.2 Prefixes referring to people

1. khon   คน   prefix for *person, people*

2. phûu   ผู้   prefix for *person, people*

3. tsâu   เจ้า   *person* prefix to show ownership, to be
                           good at something or to show continuity

4. tʃaau   ชาว   prefix for *persons*

- Here **khon** คน *person* is placed before the adjective **ruuai** รวย *to be rich*. The meaning becomes *rich people*.

19.2.1 khon คน *person* prefix refers to persons and people
Example:

> *khon-ruuai* mii ngən yɔ́ คน รวย มี เงิน เยอะ
> *person-rich* have money much
> *Rich people have a lot of money.*

khon-dii	คน ดี	*good person*
khon-rák	คน รัก	*darling, lover*
khon-khàp	คน ขับ	*driver*
khon-ruuai	คน รวย	*the rich*
khon-ráai	คน ร้าย	*criminal*
khon-too	คน โต	*first born*
khon-ɯ̀ɯn	คน อื่น	*others*
khon-diiau	คน เดียว	*alone*

19.2.2 phûu ผู้ *person* prefix refers to persons and people
Example:

> phɯ̂ɯan phǒm pen *phûu-tsàt-kaan* เพื่อน ผม เป็น ผู้ จัด การ
> friend I be *person-arrange-task* – *My friend is a manager.*

- Here we have placed the prefix **phûu** ผู้ *person* before the verb
tsàt-kaan จัด การ *to manage.* **phûu-tsàt-kaan** ผู้ จัด การ becomes
a noun, *manager.*

phûu-tʃûuai	ผู้ ช่วย	*helper*
phûu-yǐng	ผู้ หญิง	*woman, female*
phûu-tʃaai	ผู้ ชาย	*man, male*
phûu-yài	ผู้ ใหญ่	*adult, senior*
phûu-nam	ผู้ นำ	*leader, chief*
phûu-tsàt-kaan	ผู้ จัด การ	*manager*
phûu-lên	ผู้ เล่น	*player*
phûu-hâi	ผู้ ให้	*donor, giver, supplier*
phûu-pùuai	ผู้ ป่วย	*patient, sick person*
phûu-tʃái	ผู้ ใช้	*user*

19.2.3 tsâu เจ้า *person* prefix refers to persons who have special skills

Example:

> kháu *tsâu-aarom* tsing-tsing   เขา เจ้า อารมณ์ จริงๆ
> he *person-mood* really-really
> *He is very moody (ill-tempered).*

- Here we have placed the prefix **tsâu** เจ้า *person* before the noun
aarom อารมณ์ *mood.* **tsâu-aarom** เจ้า อารมณ์ becomes an adjective, *to be moody, ill-tempered.*

tsâu-tʃúu	เจ้า ชู้	*playboy (casanova)*
tsâu-khwaam-khít	เจ้า ความ คิด	*man with ideas*
tsâu-nâa-thîi	เจ้า หน้า ที่	*worker, staff*
tsâu-phánák-ngaan	เจ้า พนัก งาน	*government officer*

tsâu-aarom	เจ้า อารมณ์	*moody, ill-tempered*
tsâu-panyaa	เจ้า ปัญญา	*wise, clever*
tsâu-rábìiap	เจ้า ระเบียบ	*to be strict*

19.2.4 tʃaau ชาว *person* prefix indicates profession, nationality, etc.

Example:

> *tʃaau-thai* tsai-kwâang ชาว ไทย ใจ กว้าง
> *person-thai* heart-wide – *Thai people are generous.*

- Here we have placed the prefix **tʃaau** ชาว *person* before the adjective **thai** ไทย *Thai*. **tʃaau-thai** ชาว ไทย becomes a noun, *Thai people.*

tʃaau-naa	ชาว นา	*farmer*
tʃaau-thai	ชาว ไทย	*Thai people*
tʃaau-tsiin	ชาว จีน	*Chinese people*
tʃaau-hinduu	ชาว ฮินดู	*Hindu*

- In many instances **tʃaau** ชาว *person* can be replaced with **khon** คน *person.*

19.3 Prefixes to describe a certain profession

Example:

> khun yàak pen *nák-bin* mái คุณ อยาก เป็น นัก บิน ไหม
> you want be *nák-fly* "question"
> *Do you want to become a pilot?*

Here **nák** นัก a *skilled person* is placed before the verb **bin** บิน *to fly*. The meaning becomes a *pilot.*

1. tʃâng　ช่าง　mechanic

2. nák   นัก   person – indicates also a certain profession with some skills

3. lûuk   ลูก   prefix indicates a certain occupation, category or a junior partner

19.3.1 tʃâng ช่าง *profession* prefix indicates skills such as technician, mechanic...

tʃâng-máai	ช่าง ไม้	*carpenter*
tʃâng-klông	ช่าง ภาพ	*photographer*
tʃâng-sɔ̂m	ช่าง ซ่อม	*mechanic*

19.3.2 nák นัก *profession* prefix indicates a certain skill

nák-khàau	นัก ข่าว	*journalist*
nák-kiilaa	นัก กีฬา	*sportsman*
nák-rɔ́ɔng	นัก ร้อง	*singer*
nák-bin	นัก บิน	*pilot*

19.3.3 lûuk ลูก *subordinate* prefix indicates a certain occupation, category or junior partner

lûuk-kháa	ลูก ค้า	*customer*
lûuk-mɰɰ	ลูก มือ	*helper*
lûuk-nɔ́ɔng	ลูก น้อง	*subordinate*

19.4 Passive voice

We introduce the passive voice here as a prefix. In many books, the Thai passive voice is not treated as a prefix. However, it feels fine to talk about it in this context.

Special prefixes to express passive voice

The Thai style passive voice is usually expressed by **thùuk** ถูก or **doon** โดน verbs. They are usually interchangeable. The passive voice is mainly used for negative actions in Thai.

Thais often prefer to express activities such as *being robbed, arrested, raped, injured,* etc. with the passive voice. In these situations, the subject usually does not have any control of the situation. In English, we place the word *by* before the agent who carried out the action. In Thai, we may use either **doon** โดน or **thùuk** ถูก.

In other contexts, **doon** โดน also means *to touch* or *to hit* and **thùuk** ถูก means *to touch, to be correct, right, cheap* or *inexpensive.*

19.4.1 doon โดน

Examples:

> **1**
> kháu *doon-tsàp* เขา โดน จับ
> he *doon-catch – He was caught.*

- This is the passive voice without an agent carrying out the action.
- The prefix **doon** โดน is placed before the main verb **tsàp** จับ *to catch.*

> **2**
> kháu *doon* tamrùuat *tsàp* เขา โดน ตำรวจ จับ
> he *doon* police *catch – He was arrested by the police.*

- Here, the agent, **tamrùuat** ตำรวจ *police,* has carried out the action.
- The prefix **doon** โดน is placed before the agent, and the main verb **tsàp** จับ *to catch* is placed at the end of the sentence.

> **3**
> kháu *thùuk* khăng เขา ถูก ขัง
> he *thùuk jail – He was put in jail.*

- we may use **thùuk** ถูก instead of **doon** โดน and the meaning is the same.
- This is the passive voice without an agent carrying out the action.
- The prefix **thùuk** ถูก is placed before the main verb **khăng** ขัง *to put in jail.*

kháu *thùuk* tamrùuat khăng เขา ถูก ตำรวจ ขัง
he *thùuk* police *jail* – *He was put in jail by the police.*

- We may use **thùuk** ถูก instead of **doon** โดน and the meaning is the same.

- Here, the agent, **tamrùuat** ตำรวจ *police,* has carried out the action.

- The prefix **thùuk** ถูก is placed before the agent, and the main verb **khăng** ขัง *to put in jail* is placed at the end of the sentence.

Chapter 20

Comparative adjectives and adverbs

We normally use *comparative adjectives* to talk about two persons or two things (not three or more) to tell whether there is a difference in quality (He is *taller than* I).

Comparative adverbs are used to talk about two actions. Then, we need to have an action verb and an *adverb* to tell whether there is a difference in the manner of an action between two persons or things (John *runs faster* than Peter).

Note that the comparison can also be made between *two groups* instead of *two persons* or *things*. (Nowadays, people are *happier than* before).

The *positive comparison* is used to express the equality or similarity between two persons or things. The English format is as...as (My house is *as big as* yours or I run *as fast as* you).

The *superlative* is expressed between one noun and a group (He is the *richest* person on earth).

In English, the comparison is expressed as follows:

- *good* > *better* > *best*

- *happy* > *happier* > *happiest*

- *expensive* > *more expensive* > *most expensive*

In English, many adjectives have irregular forms such as *good* > *better* > *best*. In Thai, all words, including adjectives, are always in basic form. So, it is actually easier to express this kind of comparison in Thai than in English.

In Thai, we use the adverb **kwàa** กว่า *more* to compare *nouns* or *pronouns* with another noun. In order to express superlatives, we use the word **thîi-sùt** ที่ สุด *most* to compare one noun with a *group*.

A. Expressing comparisons with kwàa กว่า *more*

A1. Using **kwàa** กว่า *more* with *adjectives*

We normally use *comparative adjectives* to talk about two persons or two things to tell whether there is a difference in quality (He is *taller than* I).

In Thai, the adverb **kwàa** กว่า *more* is used to compare *one noun* with *another noun* (not three or more). However, the two items can be a group. In English, we need to add the word *than* in order to be correct (*bigger than, more beautiful than,* etc.).

It is good to know that in Thai adjectives can also play the role of a verb. So, in Thai we can say *"he good more I"* while in English we need to say *"he is better than I"*.

kwàa กว่า *more* normally comes after an adjective; it can be used with most adjectives.

Examples:

> kháu *dii kwàa* tʃán เขา ดี กว่า ฉัน
> he *good more* I – *He is better than I.*

- The adjective **dii** ดี *to be good* also plays the role of a verb here.
- We compare two pronouns **kháu** เขา *he* with **tʃán** ฉัน *I* with the adverb **kwàa** กว่า *more.*
- **dii kwàa** ดี กว่า is translated into English as *to be better than...*

> ② nǎngsǔu-lêm níi *phɛɛng kwàa* lêm nán
> หนังสือ เล่ม นี้ แพง กว่า เล่ม นั้น
> book-copy this *expensive more* copy that
> *This book is more expensive than that book.*

- The adjective **phɛɛng** แพง *to be expensive* also plays the role of a verb here.

- We compare two nouns **năngsɯ̆ɯ-lêm níi** หนังสือ เล่ม นี้ *this book* and **lêm nán** เล่ม นั้น *that book* with the adverb **kwàa** กว่า *more.*

- **phɛɛng kwàa** แพง กว่า is translated into English as *to be more expensive than...*

> **3** khon-tʃonnábòt *mii-khwaam-sùk kwàa* khon-krungthêep
> คน ชนบท มี ความ สุข กว่า คน กรุงเทพ
> person countryside *have-matter-happiness* more person-Bangkok
> *The country people are happier than people in Bangkok.*

- The adjective **mii-khwaam-sùk** มี ความ สุข *to be happy* also plays the role of a verb here.

- We compare two nouns (groups) **khon-tʃonnábòt** คน ชนบท *country people* and **khon-krungthêep** คน กรุงเทพ *people in Bangkok* with the adverb **kwàa** กว่า *more.*

- **mii-khwaam-sùk kwàa** มี ความ สุข กว่า is translated into English as *to be happier than...*

A2. Using **kwàa** กว่า *more* with adverbs

Adverbs often modify verbs. Normally, we use *comparative adverbs* to talk about two actions. The comparison is made between *people, animals, things, places* and *groups, etc.* or pronouns such as *I, she/ he, you, we, etc.* (John *runs faster than* Peter).

It is good to know that in Thai, adjectives can also play the role of a *verb* or an *adverb.* In Thai, it is normally enough to include an adjective after the *main verb;* hence, the adjective becomes an adverb. So, in Thai we can say *"she walk beautiful more I",* but in English we need to say *"she walks more beautifully than I".*

Comparative adverbs can also be used to talk about two groups instead of two persons or things.

In Thai, the adverb **kwàa** กว่า *more* is used to compare *one action* with *another action*. **kwàa** กว่า *more* can be used with most adjectives and some adverbs such as *much, few, less...* In Thai, when an adjective is placed after the main verb, it automatically becomes an adverb.

Examples:

nók-kêɛu *phûut* phaasăa-thai *dii kwàa* nók-krátsɔ̀ɔk
นก แก้ว พูด ภาษา ไทย ดี กว่า นก กระจอก
bird-glass *speak* language-thai *good more* bird sparrow
Parrots speak better Thai than sparrows.

- The action verb is **phûut** พูด *to speak*. It is placed before the adjective **dii** ดี *to be good* which also plays the role of an *adverb* here, *better.*

- We compare **nók-kêɛu** นก แก้ว *parrot* and **nók-krátsɔ̀ɔk** นก กระจอก *sparrow* with the conjunction word **kwàa** กว่า *more.*

- **phûut dii kwàa** พูด ดี กว่า is translated into English as *to speak better than...*

mɛɛu *wîng reu kwàa* nŭu   แมว วิ่ง เร็ว กว่า หนู
cat *run fast more* mouse – *Cats run faster than mice.*

- The action verb is **wîng** วิ่ง *to run*. It is placed before the adjective **reu** เร็ว *to be fast* which also plays the role of an *adverb* here, *faster.*

- We compare **mɛɛu** แมว *cat* and **nŭu** หนู *mouse* with the adverb **kwàa** กว่า *more.*

- **wîng reu kwàa** วิ่ง เร็ว กว่า is translated into English as *to run faster than...*

kháu *nɔɔn mâak kwàa* tʃán เขา นอน มาก กว่า ฉัน
he *sleep much more* I – *He sleeps more than I do.*

- The action verb is **nɔɔn** นอน *to sleep*. It is placed before the adverb **mâak** มาก *much* which also plays the role of an *adverb* here, *more*.
- We compare **kháu** เขา *he* and **tʃán** ฉัน *I* with the adverb **kwàa** กว่า *more*.
- **nɔɔn mâak kwàa** นอน มาก กว่า is translated into English as *to sleep more than...*

 tʃán *kin nɔ́ɔi kwàa* kháu ฉัน กิน น้อย กว่า เขา
I *eat little more* he – *I eat less than he does.*

- The action verb is **kin** กิน *to eat*. It is placed before the adjective **nɔ́ɔi** น้อย *to be few* (not much) which also plays the role of an *adverb* here, *less*.
- We compare **tʃán** ฉัน *I* and **kháu** เขา *he* with the adverb **kwàa** กว่า *more*.
- **kin nɔ́ɔi kwàa** กิน น้อย กว่า is translated into English as *to eat less than...*
- The literal translation of **nɔ́ɔi kwàa** น้อย กว่า *few more* means *more of few* (becomes *less than* in English).

A3. Conclusion

It is good to keep in mind that the comparison is made grammatically differently with adverbs compared to adjectives. In Thai, we use the adverb **kwàa** กว่า *more* in both cases, however.

Examples:

 kháu *dii kwàa* tʃán เขา ดี กว่า ฉัน
he *good more* I – *He is better than I.*

- Here, we compare **kháu** เขา *he* and **tʃán** ฉัน *I* with the adverb **kwàa** กว่า *more*. The adjective **dii** ดี *good* also plays the role of a *verb* here, *to be good.*

> **2**
> kháu *tham-ngaan dii kwàa* tʃán   เขา ทำ งาน ดี กว่า ฉัน
> he *do-work good more* I – *He works better than I.*

- In this sentence, the adverb **kwàa** กว่า *more* is used in the similar way. Compared to the sentence 1, the difference here is that the adjective **dii** ดี *good* now plays the role of an *adverb*. This sentence has a main verb **tham-ngaan** ทำ งาน *to work*.

> **3**
> kháu *dii kwàa* tʃán *mâak*   เขา ดี กว่า ฉัน มาก
> he *good more* I *much* – *He is much better than I.*

> **4**
> kháu *tham-ngaan dii kwàa* tʃán *nít-nɔ̀i*
> เขา ทำ งาน ดี กว่า ฉัน นิด หน่อย
> he *do-work good more* I *little*
> *He works a little bit better than I.*

- The comparative adverbs can also be modified with adverbs like **mâak** มาก *much, a lot* (sentence 3) or **nít-nɔ̀i** นิด หน่อย *a little bit* (sentence 4) in order to increase or decrease the degree of comparison.

A4. More ways to use **kwàa** กว่า *more*

> **I**
> kháu *kèng kwàa* tʃán *ìik*   เขา เก่ง กว่า ฉัน อีก
> he *better more* I *again* – *He is even better than I.*

- Here we have placed the adverb **ìik** อีก *more, again* at the end of the sentence.

- The comparison is between **kháu** เขา *he* and **tʃán** ฉัน *I*.

- The English translation becomes *even better*.

---

2 an-níi *lék kəən kwàa* thîi tsà sài
อัน นี้ เล็ก เกิน กว่า ที่ จะ ใส่
piece-this s*mall excess more* that wear
This one is too small to put on (to wear).

- Here we have placed the adverb **kəən** เกิน *excessive, too much* after the adjective **lék** เล็ก *small* and before the adverb **kwàa** กว่า *more*.

- The comparison is between the *size* and *to wear*.

- The English translation becomes *too small to wear.*

---

3 man *phɛɛng kwàa yɔ́* มัน แพง กว่า เยอะ
it *expensive more much – It is a lot more expensive.*

- Here we have placed the adverb **yɔ́** เยอะ *much, much more* after the adverb **kwàa** กว่า *more* at the end of the sentence.

- What is being compared is understood from the context here.

- The English translation becomes *much more* or *a lot more.*

---

4 khrai *sǔung kwàa kan* ใคร สูง กว่า กัน
who *tall more together – Who is taller?*

- Here we have placed the adverb **kan** กัน *together, jointly* after the adverb **kwàa** กว่า *more* at the end of the sentence.

- Who is being compared is understood from the context here.

- In questions, **kan** กัน *together, jointly* is commonly used with comparative adjectives.

B. Expressing comparisons with kwàa กว่า *more* referring to time

Comparative adjectives or *adverbs* can be used to talk about a person or thing to tell whether there is a difference in quality or manner in action in relation to time.

In English we say: *He is taller than before* (comparative adjective + time) or *Nowadays, he works harder than before* (comparative adverb + time).

B1. Using **kwàa** กว่า *more* with *adjectives* in relation to time.

Comparative adjectives modify nouns such as *train, bird, food, etc.* and pronouns *I, you, he, etc.* Here, they tell more about the quality of something in relation to time.

We normally use following time expressions:

kwàa dəəm	กว่า เดิม	than previously
kwàa mûua-kòon	กว่า เมื่อ ก่อน	than before
kwàa thîi-khəəi	กว่า ที่ เคย	than used to, than ever
kwàa pii thîi-lέεu*	กว่า ปี ที่ แล้ว	than last year

* We may also specify any time such as *last year, yesterday, two hours ago*, etc.

- **khûn** ขึ้น *to become more, to go up* and **long** ลง *to become less, to go down* with adverbs

- These two verbs are used in special ways in Thai. See the sentences 3 and 4 below.

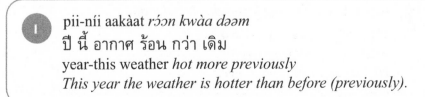

pii-níi aakàat *ròon kwàa dəəm*
ปี นี้ อากาศ ร้อน กว่า เดิม
year-this weather *hot more previously*
This year the weather is hotter than before (previously).

- **rɔ́ɔn** ร้อน *to be hot* is an adjective which also plays the role of a verb here.

- We compare the noun **aakàat** อากาศ *weather* and the time with **dɔɔm** เดิม *previously*.

- **rɔ́ɔn kwàa dɔɔm** ร้อน กว่า เดิม is translated into English as *to be hotter than previously*.

1.1

pii-níi aakàat *rɔ́ɔn kwàa pii thîi-lέεu*
ปี นี้ อากาศ ร้อน กว่า ปี ที่ แล้ว
year-this weather *hot more year last already*
This year the weather is hotter than last year.

- If we use the exact time such as **pii thîi-lέεu** ปี ที่ แล้ว *last year*, the translation changes accordingly.

2

ngaan kháu *dii nɔ́ɔi long kwàa mûua-kɔ̀ɔn*
งาน เขา ดี น้อย ลง กว่า เมื่อ ก่อน
work he *good little down more when-before*
His work is not as good as before.

- **dii** ดี *to be good* is an adjective which also plays the role of a verb here.

- We compare the noun **ngaan kháu** งาน เขา *his work* and the time **mûua-kɔ̀ɔn** เมื่อ ก่อน *before* with the verb **long** *to go down*.

- **dii nɔ́ɔi long kwàa** ดี น้อย ลง กว่า is translated into English as *less good than...* (not as good as)

3

ngaan kháu *yêε long kwàa thîi-khəəi mâak*
งาน เขา แย่ ลง กว่า ที่ เคย มาก
work he *bad down more that-used to*
His work is worse than ever.

- The adjective **yɛ̂ɛ** แย่ *to be bad* also plays the role of a verb here.

- We compare the noun **ngaan kháu** งาน เขา *his work* and the time **thîi-khǝǝi** ที่ เคย *ever* (used to) with the verb **long** ลง *to go down*.

- **yɛ̂ɛ long kwàa** แย่ ลง กว่า is translated into English as *to be worse than...*

3.1　ngaan kháu *yɛ̂ɛ kwàa thîi-khǝǝi mâak*
งาน เขา แย่ กว่า ที่ เคย มาก
work he *bad more that-used to very*
His work is much worse than ever.

- We could also drop the verb **long** ลง *to go down* and use the structure **yɛ̂ɛ kwàa** แย่ กว่า *worse* (bad more). The translation into English would be the same as in the sentence 3.

4　tɔɔn-níi kháu *kèng khûn kwàa thîi-khǝǝi* lɛ́ɛu
ตอน นี้ เขา เก่ง ขึ้น กว่า ที่ เคย แล้ว
at-this he *skilled up more that-used to*
Nowadays, he is already more skilful than he used to be.

- The adjective **kèng** เก่ง *to be skilful* also plays the role of a verb here.

- We compare the pronoun **kháu** เขา *he* and the time **thîi-khǝǝi** ที่ เคย *used to* (ever) with the verb **khûn** ขึ้น *to go up*.

- **kèng khûn kwàa** เก่ง ขึ้น กว่า is translated into English as *to be more skilful than...*

B2. Using **kwàa** กว่า *more* with *adverbs* in relation to time

Comparative adverbs modify verbs. They tell more about the action in relation to time here.

We normally use following time expressions:

kwàa-dəəm	กว่า เดิม	*than previously*
kwàa mûua-kɔ̀ɔn	เมื่อ ก่อน	*than before*
kwàa-thîi-khəəi	กว่า ที่ เคย	*more than ever* (*more than used to*)
kwàa pii thîi-lɛ́ɛu*	กว่า ปี ที่ แล้ว	*than last year*

* We may also specify any time such as *last year, yesterday, two hours ago*, etc.

- These two verbs are used in special ways in Thai. They indicate a change with adjevtives and adverbs. See the sentences below.

- **khûn** ขึ้น *to become more, to go up* and **long** ลง *to become less, to go down* with adverbs.

Examples:

> **I** sùnàk lék tuua níi *hàu yɛ̂ɛ long kwàa dəəm*
> สุนัข เล็ก ตัว นี้ เห่า แย่ ลง กว่า เดิม
> dog small body this *bark bad down more previous*
> *This small dog barks worse than before (previously).*

- The action is **hàu** เห่า *to bark*. It is placed before the adverb **yɛ̂ɛ long** แย่ ลง *worse* which also plays the role of an *adverb* here, *worse*.

- We compare the noun **sùnàk** สุนัข *dog* and the time with **kwàa dəəm** กว่า เดิม *than previously*.

- **hàu yɛ̂ɛ long kwàa dəəm** เห่า แย่ ลง กว่า เดิม is best translated into English as *to bark worse than before*.

> **1.1** sùnàk lék tuua níi *hàu yɛ̂ɛ khûn kwàa mûua-kɔ̀ɔn*
> สุนัข เล็ก ตัว นี้ เห่า แย่ ขึ้น กว่า เมื่อ ก่อน.
> dog small body this *bark bad up more before*
> *This small dog barks worse than before.*

1.2 sùnàk lék tuua níi *hàu yêɛ khûn kwàa thîi-khəəi*
สุนัข เล็ก ตัว นี้ เห่า แย่ ขึ้น กว่า ที่ เคย.
dog small body this *bark bad up more used to*
This small dog barks worse than it used to.

- We could use **mûɯa-kɔ̀ɔn** เมื่อ ก่อน *before* or **thîi-khəəi** ที่ เคย *used to* instead of **dəəm** เดิม *previous.*

- We can also change **yêɛ long** แย่ ลง *(bad down)* to **yêɛ khûn** แย่ ขึ้น *(bad up).*

- So, **yêɛ long** แย่ ลง *worse* and **yêɛ khûn** แย่ ขึ้น *worse* has the same meaning in Thai.

- The translation into English would be the same or very similar in the sentences 1, 1.1 and 1.2.

1.3 sùnàk lék tuua níi *hàu yêɛ khûn kwàa pii thîi-lɛ́ɛu*
สุนัข เล็ก ตัว นี้ เห่า แย่ ขึ้น กว่า ปี ที่ แล้ว.
dog small body this *bark bad up more year that already*
This small dog barks worse than last year.

- If we use the exact time such as **pii thîi-lɛ́ɛu** ปี ที่ แล้ว *last year,* the translation changes accordingly.

B3. Conclusion

- Note that the adverb **kwàa** กว่า *more* is used in the following sentences since we have included one of these adverbs to specify the time.

kwàa dəəm	กว่า เดิม	*than previously*
kwàa mûɯa-kɔ̀ɔn	กว่า เมื่อ ก่อน	*than before*
kwàa thîi-khəəi	กว่า ที่ เคย	*than used to, than ever*
kwàa pii thîi-lɛ́ɛu	กว่า ปี ที่ แล้ว	*than last year*

Examples:

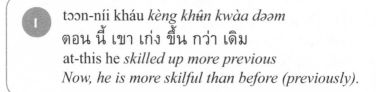

> **I** tɔɔn-níi kháu *kèng khɯ̂n kwàa dəəm*
> ตอน นี้ เขา เก่ง ขึ้น กว่า เดิม
> at-this he *skilled up more previous*
> *Now, he is more skilful than before (previously).*

- Note that the word **kwàa** กว่า *more* is used here since we have included **dəəm** เดิม *previously* to compare it with the present time.

> **1.1** tɔɔn-níi kháu *kèng khɯ̂n*   ตอน นี้ เขา เก่ง ขึ้น
> at-this he *skilled up – Now, he is more skilful.*

- In this sentence, **kwàa** กว่า *more* is not used in Thai even though the comparative form is *more skilful* in English. In Thai, we use instead the verb **khɯ̂n** ขึ้น *to go up* alone here. See also the section C below.

B4. More ways to use **kwàa** กว่า *more* and the time

Examples:

> **I** tɔɔn-níi *nâa-bɯ̀ɯa kwàa tɔɔn-nán*
> ตอน นี้ น่า เบื่อ กว่า ตอน นั้น
> at-this *nâa-boring more at-that*
> *Now, it is more boring than at that time.*

- **tɔɔn-nán** ตอน นั้น is another way to express the time in the past.
- We compare **tɔɔn-níi** ตอน นี้ *now* and **tɔɔn-nán** ตอน นั้น *then*.

> **2** phǒm yùu mɯɯang-thai dâai *sìp pii kwàa lɛ́ɛu*
> ผม อยู่ เมือง ไทย ได้ สิบ ปี กว่า แล้ว
> I stay state-thai get *ten year more already*
> *I have stayed in Thailand more than ten years already.*

- Here **kwàa** กว่า *more* is used a bit differently.

- **sìp pii kwàa** สิบ ปี กว่า is translated into English as *more than 10 years* (not yet 11).

---

3 rót-fai tsà maa-thŭng *sìp moong kwàa-kwàa*
รถ ไฟ จะ มา ถึง สิบ โมง กว่าๆ
car-fire will come-arrive *ten hour more-more*
The train will arrive soon after (a little over) ten in the morning.

- **kwàa** กว่า *more* is used here with the clock time. By doubling the adverb **kwàa** กว่า *more* > **kwàa-kwàa** กว่าๆ the meaning becomes *a little over.*

- **sìp moong kwàa-kwàa** สิบ โมง กว่าๆ is translated into English as *a little over ten in the morning.*

C. Comparison with khûn ขึ้น *to become more, to go up* and long ลง *to become less, to go down*

In Thai, the verbs **khûn** ขึ้น *to go up* and **long** ลง *to go down* are often used without **kwàa** กว่า *more.* When the time (before, earlier, at that time, etc.) is understood from the context, we cannot use the word **kwàa** กว่า *more* with comparative *adjectives* or *adverbs.*

C1. Using **khûn** ขึ้น *to go up* and **long** ลง *to go down* with *adjectives*

Comparative adjectives modify nouns such as *train, bird, food, etc.* and pronouns *I, you, he, etc.*

Examples:

---

1 thúk-wan tʃán *mân-tsai khûn* ทุก วัน ฉัน มั่น ใจ ขึ้น
every-day I *certain-heart up*
Everyday, I am getting more and more confident.

- The adjective **mân-tsai** มั่น ใจ *to be confident* also plays the role of a verb here.

- We compare the pronoun **ʧán** วัน *I* and the time with the verb **khûn** ขึ้น *to go up.*

- **mân-tsai khûn** มั่น ใจ ขึ้น is translated into English as *to become more confident.*

- Note that we cannot use the word **kwàa** กว่า *more* here since the time period (before, earlier, etc.) is understood from the context.

---

2   ngaan kháu *yêɛ khûn* mâak   งาน เขา แย่ ขึ้น มาก
      work he *bad up* very
      His work is getting worse and worse.

- The adjective **yêɛ** แย่ *to be bad* also plays the role of a verb here.

- We compare the noun **ngaan kháu** งาน เขา *his work* and the passing time with the verb **khûn** ขึ้น *to go up, to increase.*

- **yêɛ khûn** แย่ ขึ้น is translated into English as *to become worse.*

- We cannot use the word **kwàa** กว่า *more* here since the time (before, earlier, etc.) is understood from the context.

---

3   ngaan kháu *yêɛ long* mâak   งาน เขา แย่ ลง มาก
      work he *bad down* very
      His work is getting worse and worse.

- The adjective **yêɛ** แย่ *to be bad* also plays the role of a verb here.

- We compare the noun **ngaan kháu** งาน เขา *his work* and the passing time with the verb **long** ลง *to go down.*

- **yêɛ long** แย่ ลง is translated into English as *to become worse.*

- Note that **yêɛ long** แย่ ลง *(bad down)* and **yêɛ khûn** แย่ ขึ้น *(bad up)* have the same meaning *to become worse.* See the above sentence 2.

C2. Using **khûn** ขึ้น *to go up,* and **long** ลง *to go down* with *adverbs*

Comparative adverbs modify verbs. They tell more about the action.

When the time (before, earlier, etc.) is understood from the context, we cannot use the word **kwàa** กว่า *more* with *comparative adverbs* in Thai.

Examples:

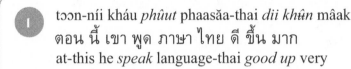

> tɔɔn-níi kháu *phûut* phaasǎa-thai *dii khûn* mâak
>
> ตอน นี้ เขา พูด ภาษา ไทย ดี ขึ้น มาก
>
> at-this he *speak* language-thai *good up* very
>
> *Now, he speaks Thai much better.*

- The action is **phûut** พูด *to speak.* It is placed before the adjective **dii** ดี *to be good* which also plays the role of an *adverb* here, *better.*

- We compare the pronoun **kháu** เขา *he* and the time with **khûn** ขึ้น *to go up.*

- **phûut dii khûn** พูด ดี ขึ้น is translated into English as *to speak better.*

- We cannot use the word **kwàa** กว่า *more* here since the time (before, earlier, etc.) is understood from the context.

> thúk-wan tʃán *tham-ngaan nɔ́ɔi long*
>
> ทุก วัน ฉัน ทำ งาน น้อย ลง
>
> every-day I *do-work little down*
>
> *Every day, I work less and less.*

- The action is **tham-ngaan** ทำ งาน *to work.* It is placed before the adverb **nɔ́ɔi long** น้อย ลง *less* which also plays the role of an *adverb* here, *less.*

- We compare the pronoun **tʃán** ฉัน *I* and the passing time with **long** ลง *to go down.*

- **tham-ngaan nɔ́ɔi long** ทำ งาน น้อย ลง is translated into English as *to work less.*

C3. Conclusion

- **khûn**   ขึ้น   *to become more, to go up*
- **long**   ลง   *to become less, to go down*

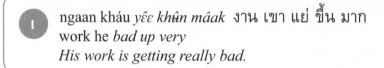

ngaan kháu *yɛ̂ɛ khûn mâak* งาน เขา แย่ ขึ้น มาก
work he *bad up very*
His work is getting really bad.

- **yɛ̂ɛ khûn** แย่ ขึ้น *worse* is an adjective in English, but in Thai, it is functioning as a verb here.

- This sentence cannot be translated very well into English directly as *He works much worse.* More correct translation would be *His work is getting really bad.*

- The adverb **kwàa** กว่า *more* is not used here since we have nothing to compare. The passing time is understood from the context.

2

ngaan kháu *yɛ̂ɛ long mâak*
งาน เขา แย่ ลง มาก
work he *bad down very*
His work is getting really bad.

- **yɛ̂ɛ long** แย่ ลง *to become worse* is an *adverb* here since we have the main verb **tham-ngaan** ทำ งาน *to work.*

- The phrases **yɛ̂ɛ khûn** แย่ ขึ้น and **yɛ̂ɛ long** แย่ ลง have the same meaning in Thai, *to become worse.* See the previous sentence 1.

3 kháu *tham-ngaan yêɛ long kwàa* ʧán
เขา ทำ งาน แย่ ลง กว่า ฉัน
he do-work *bad down more* I
His work is worse than mine.

- The adverb **kwàa** กว่า *more* is used here since we have compared **kháu** เขา *he* with the pronoun **ʧán** ฉัน *I*.

4 kháu *tham-ngaan yêɛ long kwàa thîi-khɘɘi*
เขา ทำ งาน แย่ ลง กว่า ที่ เคย
he do-work *bad down more* that used to
His work is worse than it used to be.

- The adverb **kwàa** กว่า *more* is used here since we have compared **kháu** เขา *he* with the time adverb **thîi-khɘɘi** ที่ เคย *before, used to*.

C4. More ways to use **khûn** ขึ้น *to go up* and **long** ลง *to go down*

khûn ขึ้น and **long** ลง are very important words in Thai. They are used daily by Thais in many different ways and contexts. Here we have a few more ways to use **khûn** ขึ้น *to go up* and **long** ลง *to go down*.

I phûuak-kháu *khûn raakhaa* ìik lɛ́ɛu
พวก เขา ขึ้น ราคา อีก แล้ว
group-he *increase* price more already
They have increased the price again.

- The action verb is **khûn** ขึ้น *to increase*. It is used here as a main verb; hence the meaning in English is *to increase*.
- We compare the pronoun **phûuak-kháu** พวก เขา *they* and **khûn raakhaa** ขึ้น ราคา *to increase the price*.

- **khûn raakhaa ìik lɛ́ɛu** ขึ้น ราคา อีก แล้ว is translated into English as *to increase the price again.*

> **2**   *kɔ̀ɔt arai khûn* เกิด อะไร ขึ้น
> *happen what up – What happened?*

- The action verb is **kɔ̀ɔt** เกิด *to happen.* **kɔ̀ɔt arai khûn** เกิด อะไร ขึ้น is an idiomatic expression, which is translated into English as *What happened?*

> **3**   thâa yàak pai – *yók* mɯɯ *khûn* ถ้า อยาก ไป – ยก มือ ขึ้น
> if want go – *raise* hand *up*
> *If you want to go, raise your hands!*

- Here **khûn** ขึ้น is used as a secondary verb in order to give the action (**yók** ยก *to lift*) more weight and direction. **yók mɯɯ khûn** ยก มือ ขึ้น is translated into English as *raise your hands (put your hands up).*

> **4**   *tòk-long* – kháu bɔ̀ɔk wâa man tsà *kɔ̀ɔt khûn*
> ตกลง เขา บอก ว่า มัน จะ เกิด ขึ้น
> *fall-down* – he say that it will *happen up*
> *OK! He said that it will happen.*

- In this sentence, these two words, **khûn** ขึ้น *to go up* and **long** ลง *to go down* have the following grammatical functions.

- **tòk-long** ตก ลง *to fall down* is used here as an idiomatic expression to express an *agreement* meaning in English *OK*. Actually, you can also say OK in Thai but the pronunciation is a bit different, **ookhee** โอเค.

- When the verb **kɔ̀ɔt** เกิด is used in the sense *to happen*, it is normally followed by **khûn** ขึ้น *to go up*.

D. Expressing superlatives with thîi-sùt ที่ สุด most using adjectives and adverbs

thîi-sùt ที่ สุด is used to express superlatives such as *most, greatest, maximum, etc.*

D1. Using **thîi-sùt** ที่ สุด *most* with *adjectives*

Comparative adjectives modify nouns such as *train, bird, food, etc.* and pronouns *I, you, he, etc.*

In English, we use the patterns such as *most famous, heaviest, fastest, etc. He is the most famous person here, this train is the fastest of all, etc.*

In Thai, when expressing superlatives with adjectives, we place the superlative adverb **thîi-sùt** ที่ สุด *most* after an adjective. It is used to compare *one noun* or *pronoun* with *other nouns* or *pronouns.* **thîi-sùt** ที่ สุด *most* can be used with most *adjectives.*

Examples:

> kháu *mii-tʃûu-sǐiang thîi-sùt* nai pràthêet-thai
> เขา มี ชื่อ เสียง ที่ สุด ใน ประเทศ ไทย
> he *have-name-reputation that-most* in country-Thailand
> *He is the most famous person in Thailand.*

- The adjective **mii-tʃûu-sǐiang** มี ชื่อ เสียง *to be famous* also plays the role of a verb here.

- We compare one person **kháu** เขา *he* and all other people in Thailand with the superlative **thîi-sùt** ที่ สุด *most.*

- **mii-tʃûu-sǐiang thîi-sùt** มี ชื่อ เสียง ที่ สุด is translated into English as *to be the most famous.*

2 kràpău bai níi *nàk thîi-sùt* กระเป๋า ใบ นี้ หนัก ที่ สุด
bag piece this *heavy that-most*
This bag is the heaviest of all.

- The adjective **nàk** หนัก *to be heavy* also plays the role of a verb here.
- We compare one item **kràpău** กระเป๋า *bag* and all other bags with the superlative **thîi-sùt** ที่ สุด *most*.
- **nàk thîi-sùt** หนัก ที่ สุด is translated into English as *to be heaviest*.

3 kháu *khîi-aai thîi-sùt* nai roong-riian rau
เขา ขี้ อาย ที่ สุด ใน โรง เรียน เรา
he *khîi-shy that-most* in building-study we
He is the most shy person in our school.

- The adjective **khîi-aai** ขี้ อาย *to be shy* also plays the role of a verb here.
- We compare one person **kháu** เขา *he* and all other persons in the school with the superlative **thîi-sùt** ที่ สุด *most*.
- **khîi-aai thîi-sùt** ขี้ อาย ที่ สุด is translated into English as *to be the most shy*. Note that in English, the adjective *to be shy* can have three different forms: *most shy, shyest* or *shiest;* they are all correct.

D2. Using **thîi-sùt** ที่ สุด *most* with *adverbs*

Comparative adverbs modify verbs. They tell how something is done. In English, we need to take care that the form is correct. We use patterns such as *most beautifully, fastest, heaviest, etc. He works the fastest in this company, Chanida walks the most beautifully, etc.*

When expressing *superlative*s with *comparative adverbs* in Thai, we use the superlative **thîi-sùt** ที่ สุด *most* in the similar way as it is used with adjectives. See the section D1. **thîi-sùt** ที่ สุด *most* normally comes after an adjective or an adverb; it can be used with most adjectives and with some adverbs.

Note that when an adjective is placed after the main verb, it normally becomes an adverb in Thai.

Examples:

> **1**
> kháu *dəən sǔuai thîi-sùt* nai lôok
> เขา เดิน สวย ที่ สุด ใน โลก
> she *walk beautiful that-most* in world
> *She walks the most beautifully in the world.*

- The action verb is **dəən** เดิน *to walk*. The adjective **sǔuai** สวย *to be beautiful* also plays the role of an *adverb* here, *beautifully*.

- We compare **kháu** เขา *she* to all the other people in the world with the superlative **thîi-sùt** ที่ สุด *most*.

- **dəən sǔuai thîi-sùt** เดิน สวย ที่ สุด is translated into English as *to walk the most beautifully.*

> **2**
> kháu *wîng reu thîi-sùt* เขา วิ่ง เร็ว ที่ สุด
> he *run fast that-most – He is running the fastest.*

- The action verb is **wîng** วิ่ง *to run*. The adjective **reu** เร็ว *to be fast* also plays the role of an *adverb* here, *fast*.

- We compare **kháu** เขา *he* and all the other people which is understood from the context with the superlative **thîi-sùt** ที่ สุด *most*.

- **wîng reu thîi-sùt** วิ่ง เร็ว ที่ สุด is translated into English as *to run the fastest.*

> **3**
> *fǒn-tòk nàk thîi-sùt* nai dɯɯan míthùnaa
> ฝน ตก หนัก ที่ สุด ใน เดือน มิถุนา
> rain fall heavy that-most in month June
> *It rains the heaviest in June.*

- The action verb is **fǒn-tòk** ฝน ตก *to rain*. The adjective **nàk** หนัก *to be heavy* also plays the role of an *adverb* here, *heavily*.

- We compare **dʉʉan míthùnaa** เดือน มิถุนา *June* and the rest of the months of the year with the superlative **thîi-sùt** ที่ สุด *most*.

- **fǒn-tòk nàk thîi-sùt** ฝน ตก หนัก ที่ สุด is translated into English as *to rain the heaviest*.

---

4 kháu *tham-ngaan yɛ̂ɛ thîi-sùt* nai bɔɔrísàt níi
เขา ทำ งาน เขา แย่ ที่ สุด ใน บริษัท นี้
he *do-work bad that-most* in company this
He is the worst worker in this company.

- The action verb is **tham-ngaan** ทำ งาน *to work*. The adjective **yɛ̂ɛ** แย่ *to be bad* also plays the role of an *adverb* here, *worst*.

- Here we compare **kháu** เขา *he* and the rest of the people in this company with the superlative **thîi-sùt** ที่ สุด *most*.

- **tham-ngaan yɛ̂ɛ thîi-sùt** ทำ งาน แย่ ที่ สุด is translated literally as *to work worst*. However, the more correct translation into English would be *to be the worst worker.*

D3. Conclusion

Superlatives are quite easy to use in Thai. Just place the word **thîi-sùt** ที่ สุด *most* after an adjective or after an adverb.

Examples:

---

 kháu *sǔuai thîi-sùt* nai lôok เขา สวย ที่ สุด ใน โลก
she beautiful *that-most* in world
She is the most beautiful person in the world.

- **thîi-sùt** ที่ สุด *most* is normally placed after an adjective; it can be used with most *adjectives*, here **sǔuai** สวย *to be beautiful*. The adjective, **sǔuai** สวย *to be beautiful,* also plays the role of a verb here.

> **2** kháu *dəən sǔuai thîi-sùt* nai lôok
> เขา เดิน สวย ที่ สุด ใน โลก
> she *walk beautiful that-most* in world
> *She walks the most beautifully in the world.*

- The main verb is **dəən** เดิน *to walk.* The adjective **sǔuai** สวย *to be beautiful* plays the role of an adverb here, *beautifully* in English.

D4. More ways to use **thîi-sùt** ที่ สุด *most*

> **1** kháu *mii* rót-yon *mâak thîi-sùt*
> เขา มี รถ ยนต์ มาก ที่ สุด
> he *have* car-motor *much that-most*
> *He has more cars than anybody.*

- The main verb is **mii** มี *to have.* The superlative **thîi-sùt** ที่ สุด *most* is placed after the adverb **mâak** มาก *much.*

- **mâak thîi-sùt** มาก ที่ สุด is stronger expression than **thîi-sùt** ที่ สุด *most* alone.

> **2** wan-tsan rau *mii* lûuk-kháa *nɔ́ɔi thîi-sùt*
> วัน จันทร์ เรา มี ลูก ค้า น้อย ที่ สุด
> day-moon we *have* partner-business *little that-most*
> *On Mondays we have less customers than on other days.*

- The main verb is **mii** มี *to have.* The superlative **thîi-sùt** ที่ สุด *most* is placed after the adverb **nɔ́ɔi** น้อย *little, not many.*

- **nɔ́ɔi thîi-sùt** น้อย ที่ สุด *the fewest* is the opposite of **mâak thîi-sùt** มาก ที่ สุด *the most.*

>
> phŏm rɔɔ naan – *nai thîi-sùt* kháu kɔ̂ɔ maa
> ผม รอ นาน – ใน ที่ สุด เขา ก็ มา
> I wait long *in that-most* he also come
> *I waited for a long time, and finally he came.*

- **thîi-sùt** ที่ สุด *most* is used somewhat differently here. The main verb is **rɔɔ** รอ *to wait*. **thîi-sùt** ที่ สุด *most* is placed at the beginning of the second clause.

- **nai thîi-sùt** ใน ที่ สุด is directly translated into English as *finally, at last.*

E. Expressing the equality in Thai using adjectives and adverbs

Expressing the equality between two nouns in Thai is somewhat more complicated than in English. English expresses the equality simply as *as good as..., same as..., similar to...,* etc.

The difficulty in Thai is that it uses several different constructions, which have the same or similar meaning. Sometimes, the difference is very subtle. It is best to learn to use these words in a sentence. They are normally translated into English as *as...as...*

In Thai, we commonly use the following conjunction words:

a) **thâu** เท่า *to be equal* (stressing the equality referring to levels and numbers, etc.)

b) **phɔɔ-kàp** พอ กับ *to be equal with* (expressing the equality when the numbers or levels are not important.)*

c) **mŭuan** เหมือน *to be the same* (general)

d) **khláai** คล้าย *to be similar* (general)

* **phɔɔ** พอ alone means *enough*. Therefore, it cannot be used alone and needs the word **kàp** กับ *with*.

We call these words simply *conjunction words* even though in Thai the classification can sometimes be difficult. The same word could also play the role of an *adjective*, an *adverb* or a *verb*, at least as far as the English grammar is concerned. All this needs some attention on your part to get the subtle differences right.

Depending on the context and the sentence structure, we may add **kàp** กับ *with* or **kan** กัน *together* after these conjunction words. We can also *double* the conjunction word to decrease the meaning; then, it is often translated into English as *about as...*

E1. Expressing the equality with *adjectives*

> With adjectives we compare one noun with another noun which are the *same* or *similar*.
>
> In English, we use the verb *to be* (am, is, are) and the pattern *as... as...* He *is as good as* anybody.

Examples:

a) **thâu** เท่า *to be equal*

> **thâu** เท่า is normally used to stress the equality referring to measurements, levels and numbers.

> kháu *sǔung thâu* mêɛ เขา สูง เท่า แม่
> she *tall equal* mother – *She is as tall as her mother.*

- The adjective **sǔung** สูง *to be tall* also plays the role of a verb here.
- We compare two pronouns **kháu** เขา *she* and **mêɛ** แม่ *mother* with the conjunction word **thâu** เท่า *to be equal*.
- **sǔung thâu** สูง เท่า is translated into English as *to be as tall as...* (to be equally tall as...).

> kháu *sǔung thâu kàp* mêɛ เขา สูง เท่า กับ แม่.
> she *tall equal with* mother – *She is as tall as her mother.*

- Here we have included the word **kàp** กับ *with* to emphasize the comparison. **thâu kàp** เท่า กับ *to be equal* (with) emphasizes the fact we are comparing *her* with *her mother*.

1.2   kháu *lέ* mɛ̂ɛ *sŭung thâu-kan* เขา และ แม่ สูง เท่า กัน

1.2.1   kháu *kàp* mɛ̂ɛ *sŭung thâu-kan* เขา กับ แม่ สูง เท่า กัน
she *and* mother *tall equal-together*
She and her mother are equally tall.

- Here we have used a different construction and placed **thâu-kan** เท่า กัน at the end of the sentence. **thâu-kan** เท่า กัน *to be equal* (together) emphasizes the fact that *she* and *her mother are equally tall.*

- **lέ** และ *and* and **kàp** กับ *and* both have the same meaning in the sentences 1.2 and 1.2.1.

1.3   kháu *sŭung thâu-thâu* mɛ̂ɛ เขา สูง เท่าๆ แม่
she *tall equal-equal* mother
She is about as tall as her mother.

- We may double the conjunction word and use **thâu-thâu** เท่าๆ. Then, the translation into English is *to be about as tall as...*

b) **phɔɔ-kàp** พอ กับ *to be equal*

     phɔɔ-kàp พอ กับ is normally used when numbers or levels are not important.

I   nísăi khun *dii phɔɔ-phɔɔ-kàp* khon-thai
นิสัย คุณ ดี พอๆ กับ คน ไทย
behaviour you *good enough-enough-with* person-thai
Your behaviour is equally good (nice, pleasant) as Thai people's behaviour.

- The adjective **dii** ดี *to be good* also plays the role of a verb here.

- We compare two nouns **nísǎi khun** นิสัย คุณ *your behaviour* and **khon-thai** คนไทย *Thai people* with the conjunction word **phɔɔ-phɔɔ-kàp** พอๆ กับ *to be about the same as...*

- **dii phɔɔ-phɔɔ-kàp** ดี พอๆ กับ is translated into English as *to be about as good as...*

- **phɔɔ-phɔɔ-kàp** พอๆ กับ *to be about as equal as* (with) is more common than **phɔɔ-kàp** พอ กับ *to be equal* (with).

> **1.1** nísǎi khun *lɛ́* khon-thai *dii phɔɔ-phɔɔ-kan*
> นิสัย คุณ และ คน ไทย ดี พอๆ กัน
> behaviour you *and* person-thai *good enough-enough-together*
> *Your behaviour and Thai people's behaviour are equally good (nice, pleasant).*

- Here we have used a different construction and placed **phɔɔ-phɔɔ-kan** พอๆ กัน at the end of the sentence.

- **dii phɔɔ-phɔɔ-kan** ดี พอๆ กัน *to be equally good* (together) emphasizes the fact that *your behaviour* and *Thai people's behaviour are equally good.*

- **lɛ́** และ *and* is used instead of **kàp** กับ *and*. Both have the same meaning in Thai here.

c) **mǔuan** เหมือน *to be the same*

   mǔuan เหมือน is used in the general sense referring to different types of comparisons.

> **I** kháu *kèng mǔuan* khon ùun-ùun
> เขา เก่ง เหมือน คน อื่นๆ
> he *skilful as* person other-other
> *He is as good as others. (He is as good as anybody.)*

- The adjective **kèng** เก่ง *to be skilful* also plays the role of a verb here.

- We compare **kháu** เขา *he* and **khon ùun-ùun** คน อื่นๆ *other people* with the conjunction word **mǔuan** เหมือน *to be the same*.

- **kèng mǔuan** เก่ง เหมือน is translated into English as *to be as skilful as..., to be as good as...*

1.1 kháu *kèng mǔuan kàp* khon ùun-ùun
เขา เก่ง เหมือน กับ คน อื่นๆ
he *skilful as with* person other-other
He is as good as others are. (He is as good as anybody).

- Here we have included the word **kàp** กับ *with* to emphasize the comparison. **kèng mǔuan kàp** เก่ง เหมือน กับ emphasizes the fact that *he* is compared with *other people*.

1.2 kháu *lé* khon ùun-ùun *kèng mǔuan-kan*
เขา และ คน อื่นๆ เก่ง เหมือน กัน

1.2.1 kháu *kàp* khon ùun-ùun *kèng mǔuan-kan*
เขา กับ คน อื่นๆ เก่ง เหมือน กัน
he *and* person other-other *skilful as-together*
He and others are equally skilful.

- Here we have used a different construction and placed **mǔuan-kan** เหมือน กัน at the end of the sentence. **kèng mǔuan-kan** เก่ง เหมือน กัน emphasizes the fact here that *he* and *other people are equally skilful*.

- Note that **lé** และ *and* and **kàp** กับ *and* both mean *and* here.

---

2 rót-fai *reu mǔuan-mǔuan* rót-bát
รถ ไฟ เร็ว เหมือนๆ รถ บัส
car-fire *fast as-as* with car-bus
The train is about as fast as the bus.

- By doubling the conjunction word, we can play down the meaning or similarity.

- **reu mǔuan-mǔuan** เร็ว เหมือนๆ is translated into English as *is about as fast as...*

---

3 mɛɛu sǐi-dam tuua-níi *nâa-rák mǔuan-kan*
แมว สี ดำ ตัว นี้ น่า รัก เหมือน กัน
cat colour-black body-this *nâa-love as-together*
This black cat is cute as well (as cute as the other cats).

- Here we have used a different construction and placed **mǔuan-kan** เหมือน กัน at the end of the sentence.

- We compare **mɛɛu sǐi-dam** แมว สี ดำ *black cat* with other cats which is understood from the context.

- In this context, **mǔuan-kan** เหมือน กัน *to be the same* (together) is translated here into English as *also, as well, too*. Thais love to use this kind of an expression in many different situations.

- **nâa-rák mǔuan-kan** น่า รัก เหมือน กัน is translated into English as *to be cute as well*.

d) **khláai** คล้าย *to be similar*

  khláai คล้าย is used in the general sense referring to different types of comparisons. **khláai** คล้าย denotes lesser degree of similarity compared to **mǔuan** เหมือน *to be the same*.

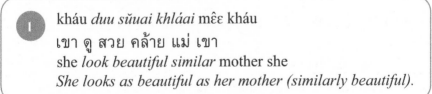

1 kháu *duu sǔuai khláai* mɛ̂ɛ kháu
เขา ดู สวย คล้าย แม่ เขา
she *look beautiful similar* mother she
She looks as beautiful as her mother (similarly beautiful).

- **duu sǔuai** ดู สวย means *to look beautiful*.

- We compare two nouns **kháu** เขา *she* and **mɛ̂ɛ kháu** แม่ เขา her mother with the conjunction word **khláai** คล้าย *to be similar*.

- **duu sǔuai khláai** ดู สวย คล้าย is translated into English as *to look similarly beautiful*.

1.1

kháu *duu sǔuai khláai kàp* mɛ̂ɛ kháu
เขา ดู สวย คล้าย กับ แม่ เขา
she *look beautiful similar with* mother she
She looks as beautiful as her mother (similarly beautiful).

- Here we have included the word **kàp** กับ *with* to emphasize the comparison. **khláai kàp** คล้าย กับ *similar* (with) emphasizes the fact that we are comparing *she* with *her mother*.

1.2

kháu *lɛ́* mɛ̂ɛ kháu *duu sǔuai khláai-kan*
เขา และ แม่ เขา ดู สวย คล้าย กัน

1.2.1

kháu *kàp* mɛ̂ɛ kháu *duu sǔuai khláai-kan*
เขา กับ แม่ เขา ดู สวย คล้าย กัน
she *and* her mother *look beautiful similar-together*
She looks as beautiful as her mother (similarly beautiful).

- Here we have used the different construction and placed **khláai-kan** คล้าย กัน at the end of the sentence. **khláai-kan** คล้าย กัน *similar* (together) emphasizes the fact that *she* and *her mother* are *similarly beautiful*.

- Note that **lɛ́** และ and **kàp** กับ both mean *and* here.

2

phûuak-kháu khîi *moohǒo khláai-khláai-kan*
พวก เขา ขี้ โมโห คล้ายๆ กัน
group-he khîi *angry similar-similar-with*
They are all angry all the same (similarly angry).
/ They seem to be all angry.

- The adjective **moohŏo** โมโห *to be angry* also plays the role of a verb here.

- We compare **phûuak-kháu** พวก เขา *they* with the conjunction word **khláai-khláai-kan** คล้ายๆ กัน *to be similar* (together). By doubling of the conjunction word, we can play down the meaning or similarity.

- **khîi moohŏo khláai-khláai-kan** ขี้ โมโห คล้ายๆ กัน is translated into English as *to be similarly angry.*

E2. Expressing the equality with *adverbs*

With *adverbs* we compare *two actions* (one noun with other nouns) which are the same or similar. One particular feature in Thai is that when an adjective is placed after the main verb, it automatically becomes an adverb.

In English, the format is a *verb + as...as: He drives as well as anybody, I work as hard as Peter does, etc.*

The difficulty here is that Thai uses several different expressions, which have a similar meaning. In order to express the equality in Thai with adverbs, we commonly use the following conjunction words:

a) **thâu** เท่า *to be equal* (stressing the equality referring to levels and numbers, etc.)

b) **phɔɔ-kàp** พอ กับ *to be equal* (expressing the equality when the numbers or levels are not important.)*

c) **mŭuan** เหมือน *to be the same* (general)

d) **khláai** คล้าย *to be similar* (general)

* **phɔɔ** พอ alone means *enough.* Therefore, it needs **kàp** กับ *with* when comparing two items with adjectives or adverbs.

Depending on the context, we may add **kàp** กับ *with,* **kan** กัน *together* or **thîi** ที่ *that,* after the above conjunction words.

Examples:

a) **thâu** เท่า *to be equal*

   thâu เท่า is used to stress the equality referring to measurements, levels and numbers.

> **I** tʃán *tham-ngaan yɔ́ thâu* khun
> ฉัน ทำ งาน เยอะ เท่า คุณ
> I *do-work much equal* you – *I work as much as you do.*

- The action is **tham-ngaan** ทำ งาน *to work*. It is placed before the adverb **yɔ́** เยอะ *much* which also plays the role of an *adverb* here.

- We compare **tʃán** ฉัน *I* and **khun** คุณ *you* with **thâu** เท่า *equal to.*

- **tham-ngaan yɔ́ thâu** ทำ งาน เยอะ เท่า is translated into English as *to work as much as...*

> **1.1** tʃán *tham-ngaan yɔ́ thâu kàp* khun
> ฉัน ทำ งาน เยอะ เท่า กับ คุณ
> I *do-work much equal with* – *I work as much as you do.*

- Here we have included the word **kàp** กับ *with* to emphasize the comparison. **thâu kàp** เท่า กับ *to be equal* (with) emphasizes the fact that we are comparing *I* with *you.*

> **1.2** khun *lέ* tʃán *tham-ngaan yɔ́ thâu-kan*
> คุณ และ ฉัน ทำ งาน เยอะ เท่า กัน
>
> **1.2.1** khun *kàp* tʃán *tham-ngaan yɔ́ thâu-kan*
> คุณ กับ ฉัน ทำ งาน เยอะ เท่า กัน
> you *and* I *do-work much equal-together*
> *You and I work equally hard.*

- Here we have used a different construction and placed **thâu-kan** เท่า กัน at the end of the sentence. **thâu-kan** เท่า กัน *to be equal* (together) emphasizes the fact that *you and I* (both) work hard.

- **lɛ́** และ *and* and **kàp** กับ *and* both have the same meaning here.

b) **phɔɔ-kàp** พอ กับ *to be equal*

   phɔɔ-kàp พอ กับ is normally used when numbers or levels are not important.

> kháu *phûut* phaasǎa-angkrìt *kèng phɔɔ-phɔɔ-kàp* khun
> เขา พูด ภาษา อังกฤษ เก่ง พอๆ กับ คุณ
> he *speak* language-english *excellent enough-enough-with* you
> *He speaks English about as well as you.*

- The action is **phûut** พูด *to speak*. It is placed before the adjective **kèng** เก่ง *to be skilful* which also plays the role of an *adverb* here.

- We compare **kháu** เขา *he* and **khun** คุณ *you* with **phɔɔ-phɔɔ-kàp** พอๆ กับ *to be about as equal as* (with).

- **phûut kèng phɔɔ-phɔɔ-kàp** พูด เก่ง พอๆ กับ is translated into English as *to speak about as well as*...

c) **mǔuan** เหมือน *to be the same* (general)

   mǔuan เหมือน is used in the general sense. It is used in many different contexts.

> kháu *khàp dii mǔuan* khon ùun-ùun
> เขา ขับ ดี เหมือน คน อื่นๆ
> he *drive good as* person other-other
> *He drives as well as anybody.*

- The action verb is **khàp** ขับ *to drive.* It is placed before the adjective **dii** ดี *to be good* which also plays the role of an *adverb* here.

- We compare **kháu** เขา *he* with **khon-ùun-ùun** คน อื่นๆ *other people* with **mǔuan** เหมือน *to be the same.*

- **khàp dii mǔuan** ขับ ดี เหมือน is translated into English as *to drive as well as…*

> **1.1** kháu *khàp dii mǔuan kàp* khon ùun-ùun
> เขา ขับ ดี เหมือน กับ คน อื่นๆ
> he *drive good as with* person other-other
> *He drives as well as anybody.*

- Here we have included the word **kàp** กับ *with* to emphasize the comparison. **mǔuan kàp** เหมือน กับ *to be the same* (with) emphasizes the fact that we are comparing *he* with *other people.*

> **2** rɔ́t-fai *wîng reu mǔuan-mǔuan* rɔ́t-bát
> รถ ไฟ วิ่ง เร็ว เหมือนๆ รถ บัส
> car-fire *run fast as-as* car-bus
> *The train is about as fast as the bus.*

- The action verb is **wîng** วิ่ง *to run.* It is placed before the adjective **reu** เร็ว *to be fast* which also plays the role of an *adverb* here.

- We compare two nouns **rɔ́t-fai** รถ ไฟ *train* with **rɔ́t-bát** รถ บัส *bus* with **mǔuan-mǔuan** เหมือนๆ *about the same as… as.*

- **wîng reu mǔuan-mǔuan** วิ่ง เร็ว เหมือนๆ is translated into English as *to be (to run) about as fast as…*

> **2.1** rɔ́t-fai *wîng reu mǔuan-mǔuan kàp* rɔ́t-bát
> รถ ไฟ วิ่ง เร็ว เหมือนๆ กับ รถ บัส
> car-fire *run fast as-as-with* car-bus
> *The train is about as fast as the bus.*

- Here we have included the word **kàp** กับ *with* to emphasize the comparison. **mǔuan-mǔuan kàp** เหมือนๆ กับ *to be about the same as* (with)... emphasizes the fact that we are comparing *trains* with *buses*.

---

rót-fai wîng *reu mǔuan* rót-bát
รถ ไฟ วิ่ง เร็ว เหมือน รถ บัส
car-fire run fast *as* car-bus
The train is as fast as the bus.

- If we use only the conjunction word **mǔuan** เหมือน *to be the same* then the translation into English is simply *the train is as fast as the bus*. By doubling of the conjunction word **mǔuan** เหมือน *same as*, we can play down the equality. See the previous sentence 2.1.

ʧán tsà *pai mǔuan-kan* ฉัน จะ ไป เหมือน กัน
I *will* go *as-together* – *I will go as well.*

- The action verb is **pai** ไป *to go*. It is placed before the adverb **mǔuan-kan** เหมือน กัน *as well, also, too* which also plays the role of an *adverb* here.

- We compare **ʧán** ฉัน *I* with other people which is understood from the context.

- **pai mǔuan-kan** ไป เหมือน กัน is translated into English as *to go as well*.

- **mǔuan-kan** เหมือน กัน *as well as, also, too* is a kind of an idiomatic expression here. It is used by Thais in many different situations every day.

d) **khláai** คล้าย *to be similar*

  khláai คล้าย is used in the general sense referring to different types of comparisons. **khláai** คล้าย *to be similar* expresses the lesser degree of similarity compared to **mǔuan** เหมือน *to be the same*.

kháu tham-tuua plὲɛk-plὲɛk khláai kàp mâi yàak tham-
ngaan ìik lέɛu

เขา ทำ ตัว แปลกๆ คล้าย กับ ไม่ อยาก ทำงาน อีก แล้ว

he do-body strange-strange similar with no want do work
more already

*He is behaving strangely as if he wouldn't like to work
anymore*

- The action verb is **tham-tuua** ทำ ตัว *to act*. It is placed before the adjective **plὲɛk** แปลก *strange*, which also plays the role of an adverb here, *strangely*.

- We compare **kháu** เขา *he* and his behaviour with **khláai** คล้ายๆ *to be similar*.

- **tham-tuua plὲɛk-plὲɛk khláai kàp...** ทำ แปลกๆ คล้าย กับ... is translated into English as *to act strangely as if...* (similar to..., about the same as...)

E3. Conclusion

Thais use these conjunction words often interchangeably depending on the context. However, there is a subtle difference on meaning and emphasis.

Often the translation into English would be the same or similar:

a) **thâu** เท่า *to be equal* (stressing equality in levels and numbers, etc.)

b) **phɔɔ-kàp** พอ กับ *to be equal* (with) (stressing equality in levels and numbers, etc. when the number is not so important)

c) **mǔuan** เหมือน *to be the same* (general)

d) **khláai** คล้าย *to be similar* (general)

a) **thâu** เท่า *to be equal*

1. rót-fai *reu thâu* rót-bát   รถ ไฟ เร็ว เท่า รถ บัส

2. rót-fai *reu thâu-thâu* rót-bát   รถ ไฟ เร็ว เท่าๆ รถ บัส

3. rót-fai *reu thâu* **kàp** rót-bát   รถ ไฟ เร็ว เท่า กับ รถ บัส

4. rót-fai *reu thâu-thâu* **kàp** rót-bát   รถ ไฟ เร็ว เท่าๆ กับ รถ บัส

5. rót-fai lé rót-bát *reu thâu*-**kan**   รถ ไฟ และ รถ บัส เร็ว เท่า กัน

6. rót-fai lé rót-bát *reu thâu-thâu*-**kan** รถ ไฟ และ รถ บัส เร็ว เท่าๆ กัน

Exercise: See if you can make clear to yourself what is the difference between the above sentences 1–6.

Tips:

- Here we have used the comparative adjective **reu** เร็ว *to be fast,* which also plays the role of a verb here.

- Use **thâu** เท่า *to be equal* for comparisons referring to levels and numbers such as heights, degrees, measurements, etc. when the measurement is important.

- Double the conjunction word to decrease the level of equality: **thâu-thâu** เท่าๆ *about as...as.*

- Add **kàp** กับ *with* before the second noun in order to place more emphasis on the comparison with another noun.

- Place **thâu-kan** เท่า กัน at the end of the sentence and use a different structure. **thâu-kan** เท่า กัน *to be equal* (together) emphasizes the fact that the two nouns *are equal* in comparison.

b) **phɔɔ-kàp** พอ กับ *to be equal*

phɔɔ พอ means *enough* and it cannot be used alone here.

1. kháu *phûut* phaasăa-angkrìt *kèng phɔɔ*-**kàp** khun
   เขา พูด ภาษา อังกฤษ เก่ง พอ กับ คุณ

2. kháu *phûut* phaasăa-angkrìt *kèng phɔɔ-phɔɔ*-**kàp** khun
   เขา พูด ภาษา อังกฤษ เก่ง พอๆ กับ คุณ

3. kháu lέ khun *phûut* phaasăa-angkrìt *kèng phɔɔ*-**kan**
    เขา และ คุณ พูด ภาษา อังกฤษ เก่ง พอ กัน

4. kháu lέ khun *phûut* phaasăa-angkrìt *kèng phɔɔ-phɔɔ*-**kan**
    เขา และ คุณ พูด ภาษา อังกฤษ เก่ง พอๆ กัน

Exercise: See if you can make clear to yourself what is the difference between the above sentences 1–4.

Tips:

- Here we have used the comparative adverb **phûut kèng** พูด เก่ง *to speak well.*

- Use **phɔɔ-kàp** พอ กับ *to be equal* (with) when numbers or levels are not important.

- Note that **phɔɔ-phɔɔ-kàp** พอๆ กับ is used more often than **phɔɔ-kàp** พอ กับ. **phɔɔ** พอ means *enough* and cannot be used alone here.

- Double the conjunction word to decrease the level of equality. **phɔɔ-phɔɔ-kàp** พอๆ กับ *to be about as equal as...* is less equal than **thâu-thâu** เท่าๆ.

- Place **phɔɔ-phɔɔ-kan** พอๆ กัน at the end of the sentence when using a different structure. **phɔɔ-phɔɔ-kan** พอๆ กัน *to be about as equal as* (together) emphasizes the fact that the two nouns *are similarly equal* in comparison.

- **phɔɔ-phɔɔ-kàp** พอๆ กับ and **phɔɔ-phɔɔ-kan** พอๆ กัน are more common than **phɔɔ-kàp** พอ กับ and **phɔɔ-kan** พอ กัน.

c) **mɯ̌an** เหมือน *to be the same*

Examples:

1. rót-fai wîng *reu mɯ̌an* rót-bát
    รถ ไฟ วิ่ง เร็ว เหมือน รถ บัส

2. rót-fai wîng *reu mɯ̌an-mɯ̌an* rót-bát
    รถ ไฟ วิ่ง เร็ว เหมือนๆ รถ บัส

3. rót-fai wîng *reu mǔuan* **kàp** rót-bát
รถ ไฟ วิ่ง เร็ว เหมือน กับ รถ บัส

4. rót-fai wîng *reu mǔuan-mǔuan* **kàp** rót-bát
รถ ไฟ วิ่ง เร็ว เหมือนๆ กับ รถ บัส

5. rót-fai lέ rót-bát wîng *reu mǔuan*-**kan**
รถ ไฟ รถ และ บัส วิ่ง เร็ว เหมือน กัน

6. rót-fai lέ rót-bát wîng *reu mǔuan-mǔuan*-**kan**
รถ ไฟ และ รถ บัส วิ่ง เร็ว เหมือนๆ กัน

Exercise: See if you can make clear to yourself what is the difference between the above sentences 1–6.

Tips:

- Here we have used the main verb **wîng** วิ่ง *to run* and the adjective **reu** เร็ว *to be fast*, which plays the role an adverb here.

- Use **mǔuan** เหมือน *to be the same* for general comparisons. **mǔuan** เหมือน is a very handy word. It is also easily understood by Thais. **mǔuan** เหมือน *to be the same* expresses wider meaning of similarity than **thâu** เท่า *to be equal* which is more exact.

- Double the conjunction word to decrease the level of equality. **mǔuan-mǔuan** เหมือนๆ *about as...as.*

- Add **kàp** กับ *with* before the second noun in order to place more emphasis on the comparison.

- Place **mǔuan-kan** เหมือน กัน at the end of the sentence when using a different structure. **mǔuan-kan** เหมือน กัน *to be the same* (together) emphasizes the fact that the two nouns *are same* in comparison.

d) **khláai** คล้าย *to be similar*

Examples:

1. kháu duu sǔuai *khláai* mÊε kháu
เขา ดู สวย คล้าย แม่ เขา

2. kháu duu sǔuai *khláai-khláai* mɛ̂ɛ kháu
    เขา ดู สวย คล้ายๆ แม่ เขา

3. kháu duu sǔuai *khláai* **kàp** mɛ̂ɛ kháu
    เขา ดู สวย คล้าย กับ แม่ เขา

4. kháu duu sǔuai *khláai-khláai* **kàp** mɛ̂ɛ kháu
    เขา ดู สวย คล้ายๆ กับ แม่ เขา

5. kháu lɛ́ mɛ̂ɛ kháu duu sǔuai *khláai*-**kan**
    เขา และ แม่ เขา ดู สวย คล้าย กัน

6. kháu lɛ́ mɛ̂ɛ kháu duu sǔuai *khláai-khláai*-**kan**
    เขา และ แม่ เขา ดู สวย คล้ายๆ กัน

Exercise: See if you can make clear to yourself what is the difference between the above sentences 1–6.

Tips:

- Here we have used the verb **duu** ดู *to look* and the adjective **sǔuai** สวย *to be beautiful* to compare her with her mother.

- Use **khláai** คล้าย *to be similar* for general comparisons in order to express the lesser degree of similarity than **thâu** เท่า *to be equal* or **mǔuan** เหมือน *to be the same.*

- Double the conjunction word to decrease the level of equality: **khláai-khláai** คล้ายๆ *about as similar as…*

- Add **kàp** กับ *with* before the second noun in order to place more emphasis on the comparison.

- Place **khláai-kan** คล้าย กัน at the end of the sentence when using a different structure. **khláai-kan** คล้าย กัน emphasizes the fact that the two nouns *are similar* in comparison.

- **khláai** คล้าย or **khláai-khláai** คล้ายๆ *to be similar* expresses the lesser degree of similarity than **mǔuan-mǔuan** เหมือนๆ *to be about the same.*

E4. More ways to express the equality with adjectives and adverbs

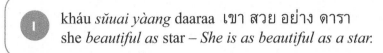

① kháu *sŭuai yàang* daaraa เขา สวย อย่าง ดารา
she *beautiful as* star – *She is as beautiful as a star.*

- The adjective **sŭuai** สวย *to be beautiful* also plays the role of a verb here.

- We compare **kháu** เขา *she* and **daaraa** ดารา *star, actor* with the conjunction word **yàang** อย่าง *as, like*.

- **sŭuai yàang** สวย อย่าง is translated into English as *to be as beautiful as…*

② thəə *sùphâap bὲεp* khon-thai เธอ สุภาพ แบบ คน ไทย
she *polite like* people-thai
She is polite like Thai people are.

- The adjective **sùphâap** สุภาพ *to be polite* also plays the role of a verb here.

- We compare **thəə** เธอ *she* and **khon-thai** คน ไทย *Thai people* with the conjunction word **bὲεp** แบบ *as, like* (style).

- **sùphâap bὲεp** สุภาพ แบบ is translated into English as *to be polite like* (style)…

③ piitɔ̀ɔ *duu mŭuan* tsai-dii ปีเตอร์ ดู เหมือน ใจ ดี
Peter *look as* heart-good
Peter looks like to be a kind person.

- The verb here is **duu** ดู *to look.*

- We compare **piitɔ̀ɔ** ปีเตอร์ *Peter* and how he seems to be with **duu mŭuan** ดู เหมือน *to look like.*

- **duu mŭuan tsai-dii** ดู เหมือน ใจ ดี is translated into English as *to look like to be kind.*

> **4**
>
> khun tông *riian yá thâu* thîi thúk-khon *riian*
> คุณ ต้อง เรียน เยอะ เท่า ที่ ทุก คน เรียน
> you must *study much equal* that every person *study*
> *You must study as much as everybody else does.*

- The action verb is **riian** เรียน *to study.* It is placed before the adverb **yá** เยอะ *much* which also plays the role of an *adverb* here.

- We compare **khun** คุณ *you* and **thúk-khon** ทุก คน *everybody* with **thâu thîi** เท่า ที่ *as much as...*which is commonly used with measurements, weights and numbers.

- **riian yá thâu thîi** เรียน เยอะ เท่า ที่ is translated into English as *to study as much as...*

- The same structure can be used with other conjunction words as well:

> **4.1**
> khun tông *riian yá phɔɔ-phɔɔ-kàp* thîi thúk khon *riian*
> คุณ ต้อง เรียน เยอะ พอๆ กับ ที่ ทุก คน เรียน
>
> **4.2**
> khun tông *riian yá mǔuan* thîi thúk khon *riian*
> คุณ ต้อง เรียน เยอะ เหมือน ที่ ทุก คน เรียน

- When **thîi** ที่ *that* is placed after the conjunction word, we need to repeat the main verb, here **riian** เรียน *to study.*

F. Expressing the equality in relation to time

When comparing the passing time, we often use **thâu** เท่า *to be equal* and **mǔuan** เหมือน *to be the same* in Thai as follows:

thâu dɔɔm	เท่า เดิม	*as equal as it was previously*
thâu mûua-kɔ̀ɔn	เท่า เมื่อ ก่อน	*as equal as it was before*
thâu thîi-khəəi	เท่า ที่ เคย	*as equal as it used to be*

mǔuan dəəm	เหมือน เดิม	*the same as it was previously*
mǔuan mûua-kɔ̀ɔn	เหมือน เมื่อ ก่อน	*the same as it was before*
mǔuan thîi-khəəi	เหมือน ที่ เคย	*the same as it used to be, same as ever*

F1. Adjectives and time

With adjectives we can tell more of a noun in relation to time. In English, we use the pattern *as...as* (*as good as before, as warm as last year, etc.*).

Examples:

a) **thâu** เท่า *to be equal*

   thâu เท่า is used to stress the equality referring to measurements, levels and numbers.

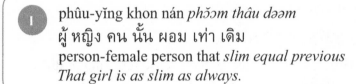

> phûu-yǐng khon nán *phɔ̌ɔm thâu dəəm*
> ผู้ หญิง คน นั้น ผอม เท่า เดิม
> person-female person that *slim equal previous*
> *That girl is as slim as always.*

- **phɔ̌ɔm** ผอม *to be slim* is an adjective which also plays the role of a verb here.

- We compare **phûu-yǐng khon nán** ผู้ หญิง คน นั้น *that girl* and the time with **thâu dəəm** เท่า เดิม *to be the same as before* (to be as equal as previously). *However,* it is better translated into English here as *as always.*

> thîi-nîi *phɛɛng thâu mûua-kɔ̀ɔn* ที่ นี่ แพง เท่า เมื่อ ก่อน
> place-this *expensive equal when-before*
> *Here it is as expensive as before.*

- **phɛɛng** แพง *to be expensive* is an adjective which also plays the role of a verb here.

- We compare **thîi-nîi** ที่ นี่ *this place* and the time with **thâu mûua-kɔ̀ɔn** เท่า เมื่อ ก่อน *to be the same as before* (as equal as before).

- **thâu dəəm** เท่า เดิม and **thâu mûua-kɔ̀ɔn** เท่า เมื่อ ก่อน are very similar when translated into English. It also depends on the context how the sentence is understood.

> **3** nɔ́k tuua-níi *mii-khwaam-sùk thâu thîi-khəəi*
> นก ตัว นี้ มี ความ สุข เท่า ที่ เคย
> bird body-this *have-matter-happiness equal that-used to*
> *This bird is happy as ever.*

- **mii-khwaam-sùk** มี ความ สุข *to be happy* is an adjective which also plays the role of a verb here.

- We compare **nɔ́k tuua-níi** นก ตัว นี้ *this bird* and the time with **thâu thîi-khəəi** เท่า ที่ เคย *as used to*. It is better translated into English here as *as ever*.

b) **mǔuan** เหมือน *to be the same*

   mǔuan เหมือน is used in the general sense referring to different types of comparisons.

> **1** kháu *sǔuai mǔuan dəəm* เขา สวย เหมือน เดิม
> she *beautiful as before – She is as beautiful as always.*

- **sǔuai** สวย *to be beautiful* is an adjective which also plays the role of a verb here.

- We compare the pronoun **kháu** เขา *she* and the time with **mǔuan dəəm** เหมือน เดิม *same as before* (same as previously). It is better translated into English here *as always*.

- Thais use **mǔuan** เหมือน *to be the same* in many different ways. It is more general and less exact than **thâu** เท่า *to be equal*.

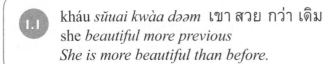

1.1 kháu *sŭuai kwàa dəəm* เขา สวย กว่า เดิม
she *beautiful more previous*
She is more beautiful than before.

- If we use **kwàa** กว่า *more* instead of **mŭuan** เหมือน *as*, then the translation changes to *to be more beautiful.*

2 phûuak-kháu *ùuap mŭuan mûua-kɔ̀ɔn*
พวก เขา อวบ เหมือน เมื่อ ก่อน
group-he *overweight same when-before*
They are as chubby as before.

- **ùuap** อวบ *to be chubby, overweight* is an adjective which also plays the role of a verb here.
- We compare **phûuak-kháu** พวก เขา *they* and the time with **mŭuan mûua-kɔ̀ɔn** เหมือน เมื่อ ก่อน *same as before.*
- **mûua-kɔ̀ɔn** เมื่อ ก่อน *before* is another way to express the past time.

2 pràthêet thai *rɔ́ɔn mŭuan thîi-khəəi*
ประเทศ ไทย ร้อน เหมือน ที่ เคย
country-thai *hot as that-used to*
Thailand is as hot as ever.

- **rɔ́ɔn** ร้อน *to be hot* is an adjective which also plays the role of a verb here.
- We compare **pràthêet thai** ประเทศ ไทย *Thailand* and the time with **thâu thîi-khəəi** เท่า ที่ เคย *as used to.*
- It is better translated into English here as *as ever.*

F2. Adverbs and time

With adverbs we can tell more about an action in relation to time. In English, we use the pattern *as...as* (*He works as hard as he used to do* or *He behaves as well as always, etc.*).

thâu เท่า *to be equal* and **mǔuan** เหมือน *to be the same* is normally used to express the equality of an action in relation to *time* as follows:

In Thai, we often use **thâu** เท่า *equal to* and **mǔuan** เหมือน *same as* as follows:

thâu dəəm	เท่า เดิม	*as equal as it was previously*
thâu mûua-kɔ̀ɔn	เท่า เมื่อ ก่อน	*as equal as it was before*
thâu thîi-khəəi	เท่า ที่ เคย	*as equal as it used to be*
mǔuan dəəm	เหมือน เดิม	*the same as it was previously*
mǔuan mûua-kɔ̀ɔn	เหมือน เมื่อ ก่อน	*the same as it was before*
mǔuan thîi-khəəi	เหมือน ที่ เคย	*the same as it used to be*

Often, the translation into English with **thâu** เท่า *to be equal* or **mǔuan** เหมือน *to be the same* have the same or similar meaning. However, there is an underlying difference depending on the context. The meaning becomes clear from the following examples.

Examples:

a) **thâu** เท่า *to be equal*

Use **thâu** เท่า *to be equal* for comparisons referring to levels and numbers such as heights, degrees, measurements, etc.

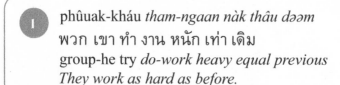

phûuak-kháu *tham-ngaan nàk thâu dəəm*
พวก เขา ทำ งาน หนัก เท่า เดิม
group-he try *do-work heavy equal previous*
They work as hard as before.

- The action is **tham-ngaan** ทำ งาน *to work*. It is placed before the adjective **nàk** หนัก *heavy* which also plays the role of an *adverb* here, *hard* (heavy).

- We compare the pronoun **phûuak-kháu** พวก เขา *they* and the time with **thâu dəəm** เท่า เดิม *as previously*.

- **tham-ngaan nàk thâu dəəm** ทำ งาน หนัก เท่า เดิม is translated into English as *to work as hard as before (previously)*.

> **1.1** phûuak-kháu *tham-ngaan nàk thâu mûua-kɔ̀ɔn*
> พวก เขา ทำ งาน หนัก เท่า เมื่อ ก่อน
> group-he try *do-work heavy equal when-before* do can
> *They work as hard as before.*

- We could use **mûua-kɔ̀ɔn** เมื่อ ก่อน *before* instead of **dəəm** เดิม *previously*. The translation into English would be the same or very similar.

> **1.2** phûuak-kháu *tham-ngaan nàk thâu thîi-khəəi*
> พวก เขา ทำ งาน หนัก เท่า ที่ เคย
> group-he try *do-work heavy equal that-used to*
> *They work as hard as they used to work.*

- We could use **thîi-khəəi** ที่ เคย *used to* instead of **dəəm** เดิม *previously* or **mûua-kɔ̀ɔn** เมื่อ ก่อน *before*. The emphasis is on *used to*.

b) **mǔuan** เหมือน *to be the same*

Use **mǔuan** เหมือน *to be the same* for general comparisons. **mǔuan** เหมือน is a very handy word. It is also easily understood by Thais. **mǔuan** เหมือน expresses wider meaning of similarity than **thâu** เท่า *to be equal* which is more exact.

> **1** kháu *tham-tuua sùphâap mǔuan dəəm*
> เขา ทำ ตัว สุภาพ เหมือน เดิม
> he *do-body polite as previous*
> *He behaves as politely as before.*

- The action is **tham-tuua** ทำ ตัว *to behave*. It is placed before the adjective **sùphâap** สุภาพ *to be polite* which also plays the role of an *adverb* here, *politely*.

- We compare the noun **kháu** เขา *he* and the time with **mǔuan dəəm** เหมือน เดิม *same as previously*.

- **tham-tuua sùphâap mǔuan dəəm** ทำ ตัว สุภาพ เหมือน เดิม is translated into English as *to behave as politely as before* (previously).

> **1.2** kháu *tham-tuua sùphâap mǔuan mûua-kɔ̀ɔn*
> เขา ทำ ตัว สุภาพ เหมือน เมื่อ ก่อน
> he *do-body polite as when-before*
> *He behaves as politely as before.*

- We could use **mûua-kɔ̀ɔn** เมื่อ ก่อน *before* instead of **dəəm** เดิม *previously*. The translation into English would be the same or very similar.

> **1.3** kháu *tham-tuua sùphâap mǔuan thîi-khəəi*
> เขา ทำ ตัว สุภาพ เหมือน ที่ เคย
> he *do-body polite as when that used to*
> *He behaves as politely as he used to.*

- We could use **thîi-khəəi** ที่ เคย *used to* instead of **mûua-kɔ̀ɔn** เมื่อ ก่อน *before* or **dəəm** เดิม *previously*. The emphasis is on *used to*.

F3. Conclusion

We make here the comparison with the following conjunction words in relation to the past time.

a) **thâu** เท่า *to be equal*

1. kháu tham-ngaan kèng **thâu dəəm**
   เขา ทำ งาน เก่ง เท่า เดิม

2. kháu tham-ngaan kèng **thâu-thâu dəəm**
   เขา ทำ งาน เก่ง เท่าๆ เดิม

3. kháu tham-ngaan kèng **thâu mûɯa-kɔ̀ɔn**
   เขา ทำ งาน เก่ง เท่า เมื่อ ก่อน

4. kháu tham-ngaan kèng **thâu-thâu mûɯa-kɔ̀ɔn**
   เขา ทำ งาน เก่ง เท่าๆ เมื่อ ก่อน

5. kháu tham-ngaan kèng **thâu thîi-khəəi**
   เขา ทำ งาน เก่ง เท่า ที่ เคย

6. kháu tham-ngaan kèng **thâu-thâu thîi-khəəi**
   เขา ทำ งาน เก่ง เท่าๆ ที่ เคย

Exercise: See if you can make clear to yourself what is the difference between the above sentences 1–6.

Tips:

- Here have used the adverbial construction **tham-ngaan kèng** ทำ งาน เก่ง *to work efficiently*.

- Use **thâu** เท่า *to be equal* for comparisons referring to levels and numbers such as heights, degrees, measurements, etc. when the measurement is important.

- Double the conjunction word to decrease the level of equality: **thâu-thâu** เท่าๆ *about as...as*.

b) **mǔɯan** เหมือน *to be the same*

1. kháu sǔuai **mǔɯan dəəm**   เขา สวย เหมือน เดิม

2. kháu sǔuai **mǔuan-mǔuan dəəm**   เขา สวย เหมือนๆ เดิม

3. kháu sǔuai **mǔuan mûua-kɔ̀ɔn**   เขา สวย เหมือน เมื่อ ก่อน

4. kháu sǔuai **mǔuan-mǔuan mûua-kɔ̀ɔn** เขา สวย เหมือนๆ เมื่อ ก่อน

5. kháu sǔuai **mǔuan thîi-khəəi**   เขา สวย เหมือน ที่ เคย

6. kháu sǔuai **mǔuan-mǔuan thîi-khəəi** เขา สวย เหมือนๆ ที่ เคย

Exercise: See if you can make clear to yourself what is the difference between the above sentences 1–6.

Tips:

- Here we have used the adjective **sǔuai** สวย *to be beautiful.*

- Use **mǔuan** เหมือน *to be the same* for general comparisons. **mǔuan** เหมือน is a very handy word. It is also easily understood by Thais. **mǔuan** เหมือน expresses wider meaning of similarity than **thâu** เท่า *to be equal* which is more exact and is normally used for numbers and measurements.

- double the conjunction word to decrease the level of equality. **mǔuan-mǔuan** เหมือนๆ *to be about the same.*

F4. More ways to express the equality in relation to time

We may also construct sentences which refer to the *exact past time, present time* or even *future time.*

Examples:

phûuak-kháu *tham-ngaan nàk thâu pii thîi-lɛ́ɛu*
พวก เขา ทำ งาน หนัก เท่า ปี ที่ แล้ว
group-he try *do-work heavy equal year that already*
They work as hard as last year.

- Here we have used **thâu** เท่า *equal* and **pii thîi-lɛ́ɛu** ปี ที่ แล้ว *last year.*

- **tham-ngaan nàk thâu pii thîi-lέεu** ทำ งาน หนัก เท่า ปี ที่ แล้ว
  is translated into English as *to work as hard as last year.*
- This sentence refers to the exact time in the past.

> **2**   phûuak-kháu *tham-ngaan nàk thâu thîi tham dâai*
> พวก เขา ทำ งาน หนัก เท่า ที่ ทำ ได้
> group-he *do-work heavy equal that do can*
> *They work as hard as they can.*

- Here we have used **thâu thîi** เท่า ที่ *as much as* and **tham dâai** ทำ
  ได้ *can be done.*
- **tham-ngaan nàk thâu thîi tham dâai** ทำ งาน หนัก เท่า ที่ ทำ ได้
  is translated into English as *to work as hard as possible.*
- This sentence refers to the *present time* which is understood from
  the context, *to work as hard as possible.*

> **3**   rau tsà *riian yɔ́ thâu thîi tsam-pen*
> เรา จะ เรียน เยอะ เท่า ที่ จำ เป็น
> we shall *study much equal-that forced-be*
> *We shall study as much as we need to.*

- Here we used **thâu thîi** เท่า ที่ *as much as* and **tsam-pen** จำ เป็น
  must, have to, need to.
- **riian yɔ́ thâu thîi tsam-pen** เรียน เยอะ เท่า ที่ จำ เป็น is translated
  into English as *to study as much as necessary.*
- This sentence refers to the future time which is understood from
  the tense marker **tsà** จะ *will.*

rau tsà *riian naan thâu thîi* thúk-khon *riian*
เรา จะ เรียน นาน เท่า ที่ ทุก คน เรียน
we shall *study long equal-that* every-person *study*
We shall study as long as everybody.

- Here we use **thâu thîi** เท่า ที่ *as much as* and **thúk-khon riian** ทุก
  คน เรียน *as everybody studies.*

- **riian naan thâu thîi thúk-khon riian** เรียน นาน เท่า ที่ ทุก คน
  เรียน is translated into English as *to study as long as everybody does.*

- When **thîi** ที่ *that* is placed after the conjunction word, we also need
  to have the verb in the second clause. So, we need to repeat the
  verb **riian** เรียน *to study* here in order to be grammatically correct.

- This sentence refers to the future time which is understood from
  the tense marker **tsà** จะ *will.*

5. Some more useful time phrases:

mûua-kîi	เมื่อ กี้	*a moment ago*
mûua-reu-reu-níi	เมื่อ เร็วๆ นี้	*recently*
tɔɔn-nán	ตอน นั้น	*at that time*
khànà-nán	ขณะ นั้น	*at that time* (formal)
sàmăi-kɔ̀ɔn	สมัย ก่อน	*former times, old days*

G. Expressing the equality directly with nouns and actions

We can express the equality between two nouns or two actions
directly *without adjectives* or *adverbs.*

What is special here is that the following conjunction words can
play the *function of a verb* in Thai.

a) **thâu** เท่า *to be equal* (with levels and numbers)

b) **phɔɔ-kàp** พอ กับ *to be equal* (with levels and numbers when the number is not important)*

c) **mǔuan** เหมือน *to be the same* (general)

d) **khláai** คล้าย *to be similar* (general)

Often, it is natural to add **kàp** กับ *with* or **kan** กัน *together* after the above conjunction words to make the sentence correct.

* With **phɔɔ-kàp** พอ กับ it is compulsory to use **kàp** กับ *with*, however.

G1. Comparing two nouns directly

We do not need to have an adjective in order to express the equality. Then, the comparison is quite general, or the meaning is understood from the context. For example, in English, we can say *she is like her mother*. In Thai, the same is expressed as *she as her mother*. In Thai, it seems there is not any adjective, adverb or verb in the construction.

In the absence of the main verb, these conjunction words can play the role of a verb similar to adjectives. That is a very special feature of the Thai language.

Examples:

a) **thâu** เท่า *to be equal*

khànàat khrûuang-níi *thâu-thâu* khrûuang khun
ขนาด เครื่อง นี้ เท่าๆ เครื่อง คุณ
size machine this *equal-equal* machine you
This machine is about the same size as yours.

- **thâu-thâu** เท่าๆ *to be about the same* is used here as a verb.
- We compare **khrûuang-níi** เครื่อง นี้ *this machine* and **khrûuang khun** เครื่อง คุณ *your machine.*

- **thâu-thâu** เท่าๆ is translated into English as *to be about the same* (to be as equal as).

> **1.1** khànàat khrûuang-níi *thâu-thâu kàp* khrûuang khun
> ขนาด เครื่อง นี้ เท่าๆ กับ เครื่อง คุณ
> size machine this *equal-equal with* machine you
> *This machine is about the same size compared to your machine.*

- **thâu-thâu** เท่าๆ *to be about the same* is used here as a verb.

- Add **kàp** กับ *with* to emphasize the comparison between **khrûuang-níi** เครื่อง นี้ *this machine* with **khrûuang khun** เครื่อง คุณ *your machine*.

- **thâu-thâu kàp** เท่าๆ กับ is translated into English as *to be about the same as, about the same compared to* (to be equal with).

> **1.2** khànàat khrûuang-níi *lé* khrûuang khun *thâu-thâu-kan*
> ขนาด เครื่อง นี้ และ เครื่อง คุณ เท่าๆ กัน.
> size machine this *and* machine you *equal-equal-together*
> *This machine and your machine are about the same size.*

- We can also use a different structure with **thâu-thâu-kan** เท่าๆ กัน which is placed at the end of the sentence.

- **thâu-thâu-kan** เท่าๆ กัน is translated into English as *to be about the same* (to be equal together).

- **thâu-thâu-kan** เท่าๆ กัน emphasizes the fact that **khrûuang-níi** เครื่อง นี้ *this machine* and **khrûuang khun** เครื่อง คุณ *your machine* are *about the same* (equal together).

- However, the translation into English would be the same or very similar as in the sentences 1 and 1.1.

b) **phɔɔ-kan** พอ กัน *to be equal* (when numbers or levels are not important)

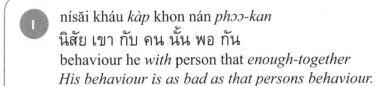

nísǎi kháu *kàp* khon nán *phɔɔ-kan*
นิสัย เขา กับ คน นั้น พอ กัน
behaviour he *with* person that *enough-together*
His behaviour is as bad as that persons behaviour.

- **phɔɔ-kan** พอ กัน *to be equal* (together) plays the role of a verb here.

- We compare **kháu** เขา *she* and **khon nán** คน นั้น that person with **phɔɔ-kan** พอ กัน *to be equal* (together).

- We could have used **lé** และ *and* or **léɛu-kɔ̂ɔ** แล้ว ก็ *and* instead of **kàp** กับ *and* to connect two nouns. The translation into English would be the same, however.

- Note that when the word **nísǎi** นิสัย *behaviour* is used alone without an adjective, it has a negative connotation in Thai. **nísǎi dii** นิสัย ดี is *good behaviour.*

nísǎi kháu *phɔɔ-kàp* khon nán นิสัย เขา พอ กับ คน นั้น
behaviour he *enough-with* person that
His behaviour is as bad as that person's behaviour.

- We could also use a different structure with **phɔɔ-kàp** พอ กับ *to be equal* (with).

- **phɔɔ-kàp** พอ กับ *to be equal* (with) plays the role of a verb here.

- Note that when the word **nísǎi** นิสัย *behaviour* is used without an adjective, it has a negative connotation in Thai.

c) **mǔuan** เหมือน *to be the same*

> **I** tʃáang-thai *mâi mǔuan* tʃáang-indiia
> ช้าง ไทย ไม่ เหมือน ช้าง อินเดีย
> elephant-thai *no as* elephant-india
> *Thai elephants are not the same as Indian elephants.*

- **mǔuan** เหมือน *to be the same* plays the role of a verb here.
- We compare **tʃáang-thai** ช้าง ไทย *Thai elephants* and **tʃáang-indiia** ช้าง อินเดีย *Indian elephants* with **mâi mǔuan** ไม่ เหมือน *not to be the same.*

> **1.1** tʃáang-thai *mâi mǔuan kàp* tʃáang-indiia
> ช้าง ไทย ไม่ เหมือน กับ ช้าง อินเดีย
> elephant-thai *no same with* elephant-india
> *Thai elephants are not the same compared to Indian elephants.*

- We may add the word **kàp** กับ *with* before the second noun in order to place more emphasis on the comparison.
- **mǔuan** เหมือน *to be the same* plays the role of a verb here.
- **mâi mǔuan kàp** ไม่ เหมือน กับ is translated into English as *not the same* (with), *not the same compared to.*

> **1.2** tʃáang-thai *lé* tʃáang-indiia *mâi mǔuan-kan*
> ช้าง ไทย และ ช้าง อินเดีย ไม่ เหมือน กัน.
> elephant-thai *and* elephant-india *no as-together*
> *Thai elephants and Indian elephants are not the same.*

- We could also use a different structure with **mǔuan-kan** เหมือน กัน *to be the same.*

- **mǔʉan-kan** เหมือน กัน *to be the same* which also plays the role of a verb.

- **mâi mǔʉan-kan** ไม่ เหมือน กัน emphasizes the fact that *Thai elephants* and *Indian elephants are not the same.*

- The translation into English would be the same or very similar as in the sentences 1 and 1.2, however.

> **2**   man *mǔʉan-kan* ləəi มัน เหมือน กัน เลย
> it *as-together* sure – *It is the same for sure.*

- **mǔʉan-kan** เหมือน กัน *to be the same* also plays the role of a verb.

- We compare **man** มัน *it* and something else which is understood from the context and from the word **kan** กัน *together.*

- Often Thais like to drop even the subject **man** มัน *it* and just say **mǔʉan-kan ləəi** เหมือน กัน เลย.

d) **khláai** คล้าย *to be similar*

> **1**   kháu *khláai* tʃán เขา คล้าย ฉัน.
> she *similar* I – *She is like me. / She is similar to me.*

- **khláai** คล้าย *to be similar* plays the role of a verb here.

- We compare **kháu** เขา *she* and **tʃán** ฉัน *I* with **khláai** คล้าย *to be similar.*

> **1.1**   kháu *khláai* kàp tʃán เขา คล้าย กับ ฉัน.
> she *similar* with I
> *She is like me. / She is similar with me (to me).*

- Add **kàp** กับ *with* to emphasize the comparison. **khláai kàp** คล้าย กับ *similar with* emphasizes the fact that we are comparing *she* with *I*.

- However, the translation into English would be the same or very similar as in the sentence 1.

 kháu *lέ* tʃán *khláai-kan* เขา และ ฉัน คล้าย กัน
she *and* I similar-together – *She and I are similar.*

- We can also use a different structure with **khláai-kan** คล้าย กัน which also plays the role of a verb here.

- We compare **kháu** เขา *she* and **tʃán** ฉัน *I* with **khláai-kan** คล้าย กัน. It emphasizes the fact that *she* and *I are similar.*

- **khláai-kan** คล้าย กัน is translated into English as *to be similar.*

- We could also replace **lέ** และ *and* with **kàp** กับ *and*. The translation into English would be the same, however.

G2. Comparing two actions directly

We do not need to have an adjective or an adverb in order to express the equality. Then, the comparison is quite general, or the meaning is understood from the context. For example, in English, we say *she works like her mother.*

Examples:

a) **thâu** เท่า *to be equal*

 khrûuang-níi *raakhaa thâu kàp* khrûuang khun
เครื่อง นี้ ราคา เท่า กับ เครื่อง คุณ
machine this *price equal with* machine you
This machine costs the same as yours.

- The action is **raakhaa** ราคา *price* (used here as a verb).

- Here we compare **khrûuang-níi** เครื่อง นี้ *this machine* and **khrûuang khun** เครื่อง คุณ *your machine* with **raakhaa thâu**

kàp ราคา เท่า กับ which is translated into English as *to have the same price, to be equally priced.*

- The emphasis here is on the *comparison* **khrûuang-níi** เครื่อง นี้ *this machine* and **khrûuang khun** เครื่อง คุณ *your machine.*

1.1 khrûuang-níi *kàp* khrûuang khun *raakhaa thâu-kan*
เครื่อง นี้ กับ เครื่อง คุณ ราคา เท่า กัน.
machine this *and* machine you *price equal-together*
This machine and your machine have the same price.

- We could also use a different structure with **thâu-kan** เท่า กัน *to be equal* (together), which is placed at the end of the sentence.
- The action is **raakhaa** ราคา *price* (used here as a verb).
- **raakhaa thâu-kan** ราคา เท่า กัน is translated into English as *to have the same price.*
- The emphasis here is on the fact that **khrûuang-níi** เครื่อง นี้ *this machine* and **khrûuang khun** เครื่อง คุณ *your machine* are equally priced.
- We could have used **lέ** และ *and* instead of **kàp** กับ *and*. Both mean the same in this context.

b) **phɔɔ-kàp** พอ กับ *to be equal*

---

kràrɔ̂ɔk *lέ* tsîng-tsòk tʃɔ̂ɔp *piin* tôn-máai *phɔɔ-kan*
กระรอก และ จิ้งจก ชอบ ปีน ต้น ไม้ พอ กัน
squirrel *and* lizard like *climb* trunk-tree *enough-together*
Squirrels like to climb in the trees same as lizards.

- The action is **piin** ปีน *to climb.*
- We compare **kràrɔ̂ɔk** กระรอก *squirrel* and **tsîng-tsòk** จิ้ง จก *lizard* with the conjunction word **phɔɔ-kan** พอ กัน *to be equal* (together).

- The emphasis here is on that **kràrɔ̂ɔk** กระรอก squirrels and **tsîng-tsòk** จิ้งจก *lizards* climb *together* or climb *in the similar way.*

> **1.1**　kràrɔ̂ɔk tʃɔ̂ɔp *piin* tôn-máai *phɔɔ-kàp* tsîng-tsòk
> กระรอก ชอบ ปีน ไม้ ต้น พอ กับ จิ้งจก
> squirrel *enough-with* lizard like *climb* trunk-tree
> *Squirrels like to climb in the trees same as lizards.*

- We could also use a different structure with **phɔɔ-kàp** พอ กับ *to be equal* (with).
- The action is **piin** ปีน *to climb.*
- We compare **kràrɔ̂ɔk** กระรอก *squirrel* and **tsîng-tsòk** จิ้ง จก *lizard* with the conjunction word **phɔɔ-kàp** พอ กับ *to be equal* (with).
- The emphasis here is on the comparison.
- However, the translation into English would be the same or very similar as in the sentence 1.

c) **mɯ̌an** เหมือน *to be the same*

> **1**　kháu *khàp* rót *mɯ̌an* khon bâa
> เขา ขับ รถ เหมือน คน บ้า
> he *drive* car *as* person crazy
> *He drives as a crazy person.*

- The action is **khàp** ขับ *to drive.*
- We compare **kháu** เขา *he* and **khon bâa** คน บ้า *crazy people* with the conjunction word **mɯ̌an** เหมือน *to be the same.*
- The emphasis here is on **mɯ̌an** เหมือน *to be the same as.*

> **1.1**　kháu *khàp* rót *mɯ̌an kàp* khon bâa
> เขา ขับ รถ เหมือน กับ คน บ้า
> he *drive* car *as with* person crazy
> *He drives as a crazy person.*

- We could add the word **kàp** กับ *with* and use **mŭuan kàp** เหมือน กับ *to be the same* (with).

- The emphasis here is on the comparison **kàp khon bâa** กับ คน บ้า *compared to a crazy person*.

- The translation into English would be the same or very similar as in the sentence 1.

> **2** tʃán *khít mŭuan-kan* ฉัน คิด เหมือน กัน
> I *think as-together – I think so, too.*

- The action is **khít** คิด *to think*.

- We compare **tʃán** ฉัน *I* and someone else which is understood from the context with **mŭuan-kan** เหมือน กัน *too, as well*.

- Often Thais drop the subject **tʃán** ฉัน *I* and just say **khít mŭuan-kan** คิด เหมือน กัน.

d) **khláai** คล้าย *to be similar*

> **1** nók-hûuk *bin khláai* nók-yìiau
> นก ฮูก บิน คล้าย นก เหยี่ยว
> bird-owl *fly similar* bird-falcon
> *Owls fly similarly as falcons.*

- The action is **bin** บิน *to fly*.

- We compare **nók-hûuk** นก ฮูก *owl* and **nók-yìiau** นก เหยี่ยว *falcon* with the conjunction word **khláai** คล้าย *to be similar, alike*.

- The emphasis here is on **khláai** คล้าย *to be similar*.

> **1.1** nók-hûuk *kàp* nók-yìiau *bin khláai-kan*
> นก ฮูก กับ นก เหยี่ยว บิน คล้าย กัน
> bird-owl *and* bird-falcon *fly similar-together*
> *Owls and falcons fly similarly.*

- We could also use a different structure with **khláai-kan** คล้าย กัน *to be similar with*.

- The action is **bin** บิน *to fly*.

- We compare **nók-hûuk** นก ฮูก *owl* and **nók-yìiau** นก เหยี่ยว *falcon* with the conjunction word **khláai-kan** คล้าย กัน *to be similar* (together).

- The emphasis here is on **khláai-kan** คล้าย กัน *to be similar* (together).

- We could have used **lɛ́** และ *and* instead of **kàp** กับ *and*. Both mean the same in this context.

G3. Conclusion

a) **thâu** เท่า *to be equal to*

1. khrûuang-níi raakhaa *thâu* khrûuang khun
    เครื่อง นี้ ราคา เท่า เครื่อง คุณ

2. khrûuang-níi raakhaa *thâu-thâu* khrûuang khun
    เครื่อง นี้ ราคา เท่าๆ เครื่อง คุณ

3. khrûuang-níi raakhaa *thâu **kàp*** khrûuang khun
    เครื่อง นี้ ราคา เท่า กับ เครื่อง คุณ

4. khrûuang-níi raakhaa *thâu-thâu **kàp*** khrûuang khun
    เครื่อง นี้ ราคา เท่าๆ กับ เครื่อง คุณ

5. khrûuang-níi lɛ́ khrûuang khun raakhaa *thâu-**kan***
    เครื่อง นี้ และ เครื่อง คุณ ราคา เท่า กัน

6. khrûuang-níi lɛ́ khrûuang khun raakhaa *thâu-thâu-**kan***
    เครื่อง นี้ และ เครื่อง คุณ ราคา เท่าๆ กัน

Exercise: See if you can make clear to yourself what is the difference between the above sentences 1–6.

Tips:

- Use **thâu** เท่า *to be equal* for comparisons referring to levels and numbers such as heights, degrees, measurements, etc. when the measurement is important.

- In these sentences, we have the main verb, **rakhaa** ราคา *to cost.*

- Add **kàp** กับ *with* before the second noun in order to place more emphasis on the comparison.

- Place **thâu-kan** เท่า กัน at the end of the sentence when using a different structure. The translation into English would be the same as when using **kàp** กับ *with* (see the sentence 3).

b) **phɔɔ-kàp** พอ กับ *to be equal*

   phɔɔ พอ means *enough* and it cannot be used alone here.

1. kràrɔ̀ɔk tʃɔ̂ɔp *piin* tôn-máai *phɔɔ-kàp* tsîng-tsòk
   กระรอก ชอบ ปีน ต้น ไม้ พอ กับ จิ้งจก

2. kràrɔ̀ɔk tʃɔ̂ɔp piin tôn-máai *phɔɔ-phɔɔ-kàp* tsîng-tsòk
   กระรอก ชอบ ปีน ต้น ไม้ พอๆ กับ จิ้งจก

3. kràrɔ̀ɔk *lé* tsîng-tsòk tʃɔ̂ɔp *piin* tôn-máai *phɔɔ-kan*
   กระรอก และ จิ้งจก ชอบ ปีน ต้น ไม้ พอ กัน

4. kràrɔ̀ɔk *lé* tsîng-tsòk tʃɔ̂ɔp *piin* tôn-máai *phɔɔ-phɔɔ-kan*
   กระรอก และ จิ้งจก ชอบ ปีน ต้น ไม้ พอๆ กัน

Exercise: See if you can make clear to yourself what is the difference between the above sentences 1–4.

Tips:

- Use **phɔɔ-kàp** พอ กับ *to be equal* referring to levels and numbers when the measurement is not important. In these sentences we have the main verb, **piin** ปีน *to climb.*

- Double the conjunction word to diminish the equality: **phɔɔ-phɔɔ-kàp** พอๆ กับ *about as...as*

- **phɔɔ-phɔɔ-kàp** พอๆ กับ is used more often than **phɔɔ-kàp** พอ กับ. **phɔɔ** พอ *enough* cannot be used alone here.

- Place **phɔɔ-phɔɔ-kan** พอๆ กัน at the end of the sentence when using a different structure.

c) **mǔɯan** เหมือน *to be the same as, alike*

1. rót-fai *mǔɯan* rót-bát รถ ไฟ เหมือน รถ บัส

2. rót-fai *mǔɯan-mǔɯan* rót-bát รถ ไฟ เหมือนๆ รถ บัส

3. rót-fai *mǔɯan* **kàp** rót-bát รถ ไฟ เหมือน กับ รถ บัส

4. rót-fai *mǔɯan-mǔɯan* **kàp** rót-bát รถ ไฟ เหมือนๆ กับ รถ บัส

5. rót-fai lέ rót-bát *mǔɯan-***kan** รถ ไฟ รถ และ บัส เหมือน กัน

6. rót-fai lέ rót-bát *mǔɯan-mǔɯan-***kan**
    รถ ไฟ และ รถ บัส เหมือนๆ กัน

Exercise: See if you can make clear to yourself what is the difference between the above sentences 1–6.

Tips:

- Use **mǔɯan** เหมือน *to be the same* for general comparisons. It is very handy word; it is also easily understood by Thais. Here **mǔɯan** เหมือน is used as a verb.

- Double the conjunction word to decrease the level of equality: **mǔɯan-mǔɯan** เหมือนๆ *about as...as.*

- Add **kàp** กับ *with* before the second noun in order to place more emphasis on the comparison.

- Place **mǔɯan-kan** เหมือน กัน at the end of the sentence when using a different structure.

d) **khláai** คล้าย *to be similar, alike*

1. nâa tʃán *khláai* phɔ̂ɔ   หน้า ฉัน คล้าย พ่อ

2. nâa tʃán *khláai-khláai* phɔ̂ɔ   หน้า ฉัน คล้ายๆ พ่อ

3. nâa tʃǎn *khláai* **kàp** phɔ̂ɔ   หน้า ฉัน คล้าย กับ พ่อ

4. nâa tʃǎn *khláai-khláai* **kàp** phɔ̂ɔ   หน้า ฉัน คล้ายๆ กับ พ่อ

5. nâa tʃǎn lɛ́ phɔ̂ɔ *khláai*-**kan**   หน้า ฉัน และ พ่อ คล้าย กัน

6. nâa tʃǎn lɛ́ phɔ̂ɔ *khláai-khláai*-**kan**   หน้า ฉัน และ พ่อ คล้ายๆ กัน

Exercise: See if you can make clear to yourself what is the difference between the above sentences 1–6.

Tips:

- Use **khláai** คล้าย *to be similar* for general comparisons in order to have lesser degree of similarity than **mǔuan** เหมือน *to be the same*.

- Here **khláai** คล้าย is used as a verb.

- Double the conjunction word to decrease the level of equality: **khláai-khláai** คล้ายๆ *about as...as*

- Add **kàp** กับ *with* before the second noun in order to place more emphasis on the comparison.

- place **khláai-kan** คล้าย กัน at the end of the sentence when using a different structure.

G4. More ways to express the equality

There are some more conjunction words we can use such as **thâu-thiiam-kan** เท่า เทียม กัน *to be equal* (on the the same level, to-gether), **duu mǔuan** ดู เหมือน *to look as*, **yàang** อย่าง *as, like* and **bɛ̀ɛp** แบบ *as, like, in the same way as*. In the absence of the main verb, these conjunction words can play the role of a verb similar to adjectives. That is a very special feature of the Thai language.

thúk-khon *thâu-thiiam-kan* ทุก คน เท่า เทียม กัน
every-person *equal compare together*
Everybody is equal.

- **thâu-thiiam-kan** เท่า เทียม กัน which is placed at the end of the sentence, is used here as a verb. **thâu** เท่า means *to be equal* and **thiiam** เทียม means *to be comparable to.*

- We compare **thúk-khon** ทุก คน *everybody* and *their situation, human status* or *human rights,* which is understood from the context.

- **thâu-thiiam-kan** เท่า เทียม กัน is translated into English as *to be equal (to be on the same level).*

---

2 kháu *duu mǔuan* mâi mii maaráyâat
เขา ดู เหมือน ไม่ มี มารยาท
he *look as* no have manner
He looks like not to have any manners.

- The verb here is **duu** ดู *to look.*

- We compare **kháu** เขา *he* and **maaráyâat** มารยาท *his manners* with **duu mǔuan** ดู เหมือน *to look like.*

---

3 sàtai kháu *bὲεp* phûu-yǐng สไตล์ เขา แบบ ผู้ หญิง
style he *like* person-female
His style is similar to women. / He behaves like women do.

- The conjunction word **bὲεp** แบบ *like, as* (style) also plays the role of a verb here.

- We compare **kháu** เขา *he* and **phûu-yǐng** ผู้ หญิง *women* with **bὲεp** แบบ *like, as, style.*

---

4 yaam khon nán *nâng yàang* yàak tsà nɔɔn
ยาม คน นั้น นั่ง อย่าง อยาก จะ นอน
guard person that *sit as* want will sleep
That guard sits as if he is going to fall asleep.

- The verb here is **nâng** นั่ง *to sit.*

- We compare two actions **nâng** นั่ง *to sit* and **nɔɔn** นอน *to sleep* with **yàang** อย่าง *as*.

- **nâng yàang** นั่ง อย่าง is translated into English as *to sit as...*

Chapter 21

tsai ใจ *heart, mind* as a prefix or a suffix

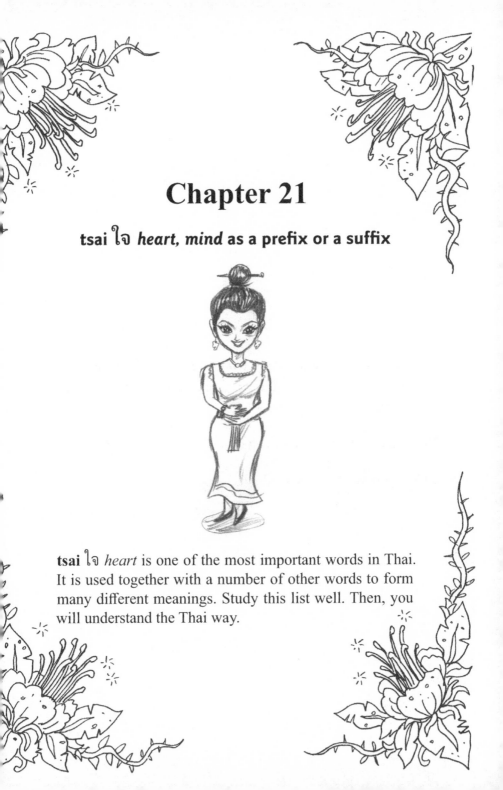

tsai ใจ *heart* is one of the most important words in Thai. It is used together with a number of other words to form many different meanings. Study this list well. Then, you will understand the Thai way.

We have saved the prefix **tsai**  *heart, mind* to be the last in this book since the subject is quite vast, and **tsai** ใจ can also be used as a suffix.

20.1 tsai ใจ *heart* as a prefix

20.2 tsai ใจ *heart* as a suffix

20.1 tsai ใจ *heart* as a prefix

As a prefix **tsai** ใจ *heart* is placed before another word, normally before an adjective or a verb. With many words **tsai** ใจ *heart* can be used as a prefix. As a result, the word combination becomes normally an adjective.

1. Adjectives such as *to be kind, generous, calm, brave*, etc.

Example:

> kháu pen khon *tsai-kwâang* เขา เป็น คน ใจ กว้าง
> he be person *heart-wide – He is a generous person.*

- Here **tsai** ใจ *heart, mind* is used as a prefix. With the adjective **kwâang** กว้าง *to be wide,* the meaning becomes *to be generous.*

tsai ใจ + dii	ดี	*good*	= *to be kind, generous*
tsai ใจ + klaang	กลาง	*middle*	= *to be in the middle*
tsai ใจ + bun	บุญ	*virtue, merit*	= *to be kind, generous*
tsai ใจ + kwâang	กว้าง	*wide, broad*	= *to be generous*
tsai ใจ + yen	เย็น	*cool, cold*	= *to be calm, cool-hearted*
tsai ใจ + tsing	จริง	*true, sincere*	= *to be sincere, honest*
tsai ใจ + rák	รัก	*to love*	= *to be in love*
tsai ใจ + pâm	ป้า	*brave*	= *daring with money*
tsai ใจ + thŭng	ถึง	*to reach, to arrive*	= *to be brave*

2. Adjectives such as *to be unsympathetic, selfish, hot-tempered, cruel,* etc.

Example:

phûu tʃaai khon nán *tsai-dam* tsing-tsing
ผู้ ชาย คน นั้น ใจ ดำ จริงๆ
person-male person that *heart-black* really-really
Really, that guy is unkind.

- Here **tsai** ใจ *heart, mind* is used as a prefix. With the adjective **dam** ดำ *to be black,* the meaning becomes *to be unkind, not nice.*

tsai ใจ + dam	ดำ	*black*	= *to be cruel, unkind, not nice*
tsai ใจ + ngâai	ง่าย	*easy*	= *to be easily influenced*
tsai ใจ + ɔ̀ɔn	อ่อน	*week, soft*	= *to be submissive*
tsai ใจ + khěng	แข็ง	*hard*	= *to be hard-hearted*
tsai ใจ + lɔɔi	ลอย	*to float*	= *to be absent-minded*
tsai ใจ + rɔ́ɔn	ร้อน	*hot*	= *to be hot-tempered*
tsai ใจ + sĭia	เสีย	*bad, spoiled*	= *to be frightened*
tsai ใจ + hăai	หาย	*to be lost*	= *to be fearful, startled*
tsai ใจ + khɛ̂ɛp	แคบ	*narrow*	= *to be narrow-minded*
tsai ใจ + tɛ̀ɛk	แตก	*to break*	= *to be spoiled*
tsai ใจ + ráai	ร้าย	*evil*	= *to be cruel, heartless*

20.2 tsai ใจ *heart* as a suffix

Suffix means that **tsai** ใจ comes after another word. It is very common that **tsai** ใจ *heart* is used as a suffix. As a result the word combination often becomes an adjective, a verb or a noun.

1. Adjectives such as *to be happy, contended, pleased, satisfied, sincere, etc.*

Examples:

> **1.1** wan-níi tʃán *dii-tsai* mâak วัน นี้ ฉัน ดี ใจ มาก
> day-this I *good-heart* very – *Today I am very happy.*

- Here **tsai** ใจ *heart, mind* is used as a suffix. With the adjective **dii** ดี *to be good*, the meaning becomes *to be happy.*

> **1.2** kháu *tsai-dii* เขา ใจ ดี
> he *heart-good* – *He is a kind person.*

- Here **tsai** ใจ *heart, mind* is used as a prefix. With the adjective **dii** ดี *to be good*, the meaning becomes *to be kind.*

> **1.3** tʃán *phɔɔ-tsai* tsing-tsing ฉัน พอ ใจ จริงๆ
> I *enough-heart* really-really – *I am really pleased.*

- Here **tsai** ใจ *heart, mind* is used as a suffix. With the adjective **phɔɔ** พอ *to be enough*, the meaning becomes *to be pleased.*

phɔɔ	พอ	*to be enough*	+ tsai ใจ = *to be satisfied, pleased*
sùk	สุข	*to be happy, pleased*	+ tsai ใจ = *to be happy, pleased*
tʃɔɔp	ชอบ	*to like*	+ tsai ใจ = *to be pleased, satisfied*
dii	ดี	*to be good*	+ tsai ใจ = *to be happy, pleased*
sàbaai	สบาย	*to be well*	+ tsai ใจ = *to be happy, joyous*
thùuk	ถูก	*to touch*	+ tsai ใจ = *to like, to be pleased*
doon	โดน	*to hit, to strike*	+ tsai ใจ = *to like, to be pleased*
tʃûun	ชื่น	*to be delighted*	+ tsai ใจ = *to be cheerful, happy*
tsing	จริง	*to be true*	+ tsai ใจ = *to be sincere*
tem	เต็ม	*to be full*	+ tsai ใจ = *to be willing*

2. Adjectives such as *to be confident, proud, surprised, sorry, etc.*

Example:

> tʃán *mân-tsai* ngaan-níi tham dâai ฉัน มั่น ใจ งาน นี้ ทำ ได้
> I *certain-heart* work-this do can
> *I am sure that this can be done.*

- Here **tsai** ใจ *heart, mind* is used as a suffix. With the adjective **mân** มั่น *to be certain*, the meaning is *to be sure, confident, certain.*

nɛ̂ɛ	แน่	*to be sure*	+ tsai ใจ	= *to be certain*
mân	มั่น	*to be certain*	+ tsai ใจ	= *to be confident*
phuum	ภูมิ	*to be proud*	+ tsai ใจ	= *to be proud*
plɛ̀ɛk	แปลก	*to be strange*	+ tsai ใจ	= *to be surprised*
pràtháp	ประทับ	*to stamp*	+ tsai ใจ	= *to impress*
dâai	ได้	*to get*	+ tsai ใจ	= *to get someone's heart*
sŏn	สน	*to be interested*	+ tsai ใจ	= *to be interested in*

3. Adjectives such such *to be uncertain, uncontended, fearful, etc.*

Example:

> phŏm *tòk-tsai* mâak-mâak ผม ตก ใจ มากๆ
> I *fall-heart* much-much – *I was really scared (shocked).*

- Here **tsai** ใจ *heart, mind* is used as a suffix. With the verb **tòk** ตก *to fall*, the meaning becomes *to be scared, shocked.*

tòk	ตก	*to fall*	+ tsai ใจ	= *to be shocked*
nɔ́ɔi	น้อย	*a few*	+ tsai ใจ	= *to be sensitive*
mâi	ไม่	*no*	+ nɛ̂ɛ-tsai แน่ ใจ	= *to be uncertain*
mâi	ไม่	*no*	+ sŏn-tsai สน ใจ	= *to be uninterested*
sĭia	เสีย	*to lose*	+ tsai ใจ	= *to be sorry, upset*

dâai	ได้	*to get*	+ tsai ใจ	= *to be arrogant**
kreeng	เกรง	*to fear*	+ tsai ใจ	= *not to offend*

* **dâai-tsai** ได้ ใจ also has a positive meaning. It can be used when you are being impressed by someone, *to get someone's heart.*

4. tsai ใจ and verbs

Example:

> tɕán *khâu-tsai* lέεu ฉัน เข้า ใจ แล้ว
> I *enter-heart* already – *I already understand!*

- Here **tsai** ใจ *heart, mind* is used as a suffix. With the verb **khâu** เข้า *to enter,* the meaning becomes *to understand.*

khâu	เข้า	*to enter*	+ tsai ใจ	= *to understand*
au	เอา	*to take*	+ tsai ใจ	= *to try to please*
hěn	เห็น	*to see*	+ tsai ใจ	= *to sympathize*
tham	ทำ	*to do, to make*	+ tsai ใจ	= *to accept*
taam	ตาม	*to follow*	+ tsai ใจ	= *to go along*
sài	ใส่	*to put on, to wear*	+ tsai ใจ	= *to pay attention*
tâng	ตั้ง	*to set*	+ tsai ใจ	= *to intend*
wái	ไว้	*to keep, to save*	+ tsai ใจ	= *to trust*
bandaan	บัน ดาล	*to inspire*	+ tsai ใจ	= *to inspire*

5. tsai ใจ and nouns

Example:

> khun pen *wǎan-tsai* khɔ̌ɔng phǒm คุณ เป็น หวาน ใจ ของ ผม
> you be *sweet-heart* of I – *You are my sweetheart.*

- Here **tsai** ใจ *heart, mind* is used as a suffix. With the adjective **wǎan** หวาน *to be sweet,* the meaning becomes a noun *sweetheart.*

wăan	หวาน	*to be sweet*	+ tsai ใจ	= *sweetheart*
duuang	ดวง	*circle*	+ tsai ใจ	= *beloved one, sweetheart*
kamlang	กำลัง	*power, energy*	+ tsai ใจ	= *moral support*
nám	น้ำ	*water, liquid*	+ tsai ใจ	= *kindness*
hŭua	หัว	*head*	+ tsai ใจ	= *heart*

Chapter 22

Words of wisdom

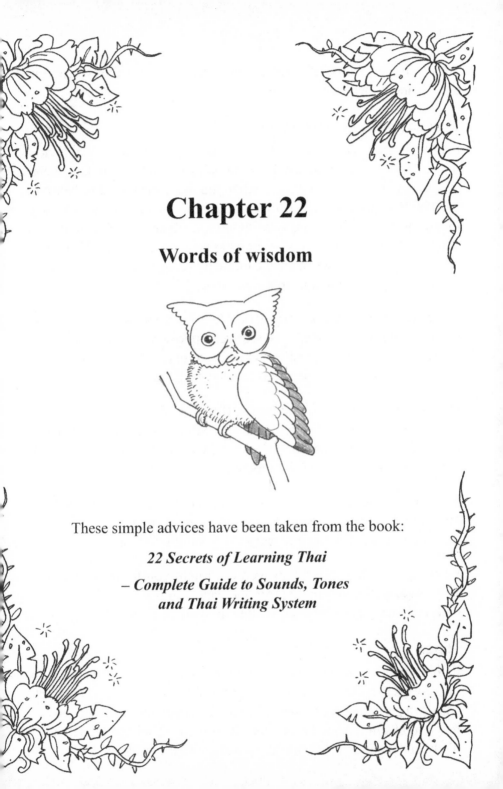

These simple advices have been taken from the book:

22 Secrets of Learning Thai

– Complete Guide to Sounds, Tones and Thai Writing System

These simple "Words of Wisdom" may prove to be useful when you are advancing with your studies.

Thai sounds and Thai script

In order to learn a new language like Thai, we need to know the sounds both in theory and in practice. If you only listen and try to imitate, there is a tendency that you will hear what you are accustomed to hearing, and therefore will not be able to reproduce the sound correctly. Correct tongue and lip positions are very important. We are no longer children, who can learn a language very quickly only by imitating. You have been speaking your own language for many years, and it has penetrated deeply into your mind and consciousness.

There are several ways to get practical help with Thai sounds. You can listen to audio material like cd's or read books with transliterations. There are also many websites, which give examples on how to pronounce Thai sounds. You can also attend Thai classes.

One way is to get a private teacher. If you do this, it is better if you know exactly what kind of help you need before you engage the teacher. Do your homework first. In other words, you need to know your weak points and then ask the teacher to help and correct you.

Be aware that learning the Thai script does not help you to understand Thai sounds any better. Sounds are sounds, and it does not matter how they are written. You need to learn every sound first, one by one.

Learning the Thai script, however, does help you to understand the Thai language in a far more profound way than if you are just relying on transliterations, which are written in many different ways.

Tones

Perhaps you will be relieved to know that Thai people themselves do not always use the correct tone when speaking. The context in which you use a particular word is very important. If you use the correct word in the right situation and pronounce it correctly, Thai people will most likely understand you even if the tone is not quite right.

Also be aware that in two-syllable words, the tone of the first syllable is often minimized and the tone of the second syllable is pronounced clearly. If you try to emphasize every tone in every syllable, your speaking will sound unnatural.

Thai people do not usually call the tones by the same name as we westerners do. If you ask the average Thai about the name of the tone, you may not get a satisfactory reply. Thai people know the tones, but are often not concerned what they are called. They are born into the habit. Moreover, in Thai, the tones are not called the same as in English. You need to use your ears while attempting to get the right tone from your Thai friends.

Three different ways to learn the tones:

Once you have learned all the sounds and all five tones properly, you can learn the tones of new words basically in three different ways.

1. By listening to native Thai people or audio files.
2. By reading the transliterated text with special tone marks.
3. By reading the Thai script for which you need to know the basics of Thai writing system and the tone rules.

In order to learn the Thai language effectively as a westerner, you might need to take advantage of all three ways.

Even though tones are a very important part of the Thai language, correct pronunciation and usage of the right word in the right situation are important as well. The right tone does not help if the word is not pronounced correctly.

Vowels

Note also that short and long English vowel sounds are not easy to describe accurately even if you are a linguist. There are many different accents, which use somewhat different vowel sounds for the same word. English vowel sounds can only give you a superficial understanding of how the Thai vowel sounds are pronounced.

While learning Thai it would be good if you could forget the English way of spelling vowels altogether, and learn a new phonetic way as shown in this book. That way, you will learn more quickly to pronounce the Thai vowel sounds more accurately.

Consonant and consonant clusters

The consonant sound **ng** ง appears in several combinations in the English language (ki**ng**, si**ng**ing, fi**ng**er, etc.). However, it can prove quite difficult for English speaking learners to use this sound at the beginning of a word. This shows how strongly language skills are based on habits. You are simply not accustomed to produce this sound at the beginning of a word.

Many Thais do not pronounce consonant clusters very clearly. So, the word **plaa** ปลา fish may sound like **paa**. The issue is further complicated since Thais often replace the letter **r** ร with the letter **l** ล or omit it altogether. Then the cluster **khrîiat** เครียด to be tense would sound like **khlîiat** or even in some cases like **khîat**, and the cluster **kròot** โกรธ to be angry would sound like **kòot** โกรธ. Understanding the meaning from the context is the key here. There is nothing else you can do.

Leaving the cluster out when speaking is widely accepted, so don't try to correct Thais. The matter is confusing for students, since in language schools you are taught the correct way, but many people simply do not speak like that.

Standard Thai uses consonant clusters in speaking as they are written. Also people of Cambodian origin in Thailand usually pronounce clusters clearly. Hence, they are often easier to understand. The words are always written correctly even though spoken differently. Because of this, ordinary Thais may experience some difficulties in finding words in the dictionary.

Please learn the correct way to use consonant clusters even if Thais may pronounce them differently. It is their privilege.

End sounds

In order to be able to speak and comprehend the Thai language properly, it is truly essential to understand the end sounds. The end sounds are basically divided into two groups, "open" and "closed" endings, sometimes also called "live" and "dead" endings.

There are less end sounds than initial sounds in Thai, since end sounds are never aspirated, and many different initial consonant sounds merge into one sound. Hence, a variety of individual sounds are pronounced the same at the end of a word or syllable.

Be polite!

Politeness is an essential part of Thai culture and language. This is something westerners need to appreciate in order to be able to communicate fluently with Thai people. Be polite in every situation with everybody at all times. It is not easy to overdo. Politeness is a built-in feature of Thai language and culture. Context is also very important, you need to be aware to whom you are speaking and where.

Persevere!

When attempting to speak Thai, take it easy and don't get upset if Thai people do not understand you straight away. Particularly in tourist areas, Thais often like to practice their English instead of attempting to speak Thai. Some Thai people need you to speak almost 100 % correctly before they can understand you. Others may understand you quite easily even if you are far from perfect.

In Thai, there are a vast number of words, which sound very similar, but the meanings are totally different. Persevere! Learn to articulate clearly and you will get it right.

Have fun!

The Thai language is "feminine". That is to say it is spoken softly. Learn to use the sounds in a relaxed way. Small mistakes are easily forgiven, but too tense and serious an effort to try to speak this beautiful ancient language correctly may give you and even Thai people a headache!

Be more concerned with 'how' rather than 'why'. For Thai people, language is a means for communication and having fun, not a complicated theory to be understood. Thai people say "right, but we do not say it like that". There is no why!

Chapter 23

Summary of some useful grammar terms

1 Grammar

In every language, we need being able to make sounds in such a way that other people understand what we are saying. We also need being able to put words together in such a way that sentences make sense and sound right. As an adult learner, this requires some conscious and active effort on your part.

When you are learning a second language as a child, you are growing into it. Learning a second language as an adult is a different process. The learning process is not that intuitive any more. Your brain also wants to understand what you are learning. If the correct way is not readily available to you, your brain will understand things in its own way. In other words, it makes assumptions, right or wrong, from point of view of your own native language. Since Thai uses a different kind of syntax to English, the assumptions made may not be valid. You need to think the way Thai people do in order to speak Thai fluently.

1.1 Phonetics

Phonetics is concerned with the sounds of the language. This is quite important since English sounds cannot be directly transferred into Thai. This is true particularly with the vowel sounds. If you want to be understood by Thais, you need being able to produce correct Thai sounds.

You can also find more comprehensive explanation of Thai sounds in the book *22 Secrets of Learning Thai – Complete Guide to Sounds, Tones and Thai Writing System.*

1.2 Transliteration

Transliteration is a way to write Thai sounds with western letters and international phonetic symbols. This helps you to get sounds right since it may take a long time for you to able to read the Thai script properly. See more about the transliteration of Thai sounds at the end of this book.

1.3 Syntax

Syntax is concerned with the structure of the language, how the words are put together in the sentence. This is important since the Thai language uses a different type of syntax from English.

1.4 Semantics

Semantics is concerned with the meaning of words and sentences. This is important since one word can have several different semantic meanings. **dâai** ได้ is a very good example of this type of word. It may change the semantic meaning when placed in different positions in a sentence.

1.5 Semantic boundary

We use the term *semantic boundary* to describe the fact that we need to use different English words in order to define the meaning of the verb **dâai** ได้. We need to use English words such as *to get, to receive, can, being permitted to, to have an opportunity to,* etc. to grasp the correct meaning of **dâai** ได้ when placed in different positions in a sentence.

2 Parts of speech

When describing the structure of the Thai language, we need to know a few basic terms, usually called in English *parts of speech.*

2.1 Nouns

2.1.1 Common nouns

The word *common noun* is a word used for things such as *dogs, cats, cars, computers.* They have a physical form and they can be touched. **dâai** ได้ can be placed before a noun in order to have a distinct meaning, *to get.*

2.1.2 Abstract nouns

An *abstract noun* is a word used for things like *luck, beauty* and *effectiveness.* These nouns do not have a physical form and cannot be touched. **dâai** ได้ can be placed before an abstract noun in order to have a distinct meaning.

2.1.3 Classifiers

Thai count nouns are called *classifiers.* In English we also have classifiers: *two bottles of milk, head of cattle, a glass of beer.* Perhaps, more accurate term for this type of nouns is "measure words". The difference is that in Thai it is compulsory to use classifiers for all nouns when counting. For example, you cannot say in Thai *two cars.* You must say *a car two vehicles. Vehicle* would be here a classifier in Thai. See Chapter 18.

2.2 Personal pronouns

Personal pronouns such as *I, he* and *we.* In Thai personal pronouns are used much more and in a wider sense than in English. They refer to age, gender, social status and the context. See Chapter 3.

2.3 Verbs

2.3.1 Main verb

When **dâai** ได้ is a *main verb*, it means *to get.*

2.3.2 Helping verb

As a *helping verb* **dâai** ได้ is placed before the main verb or after it. More information can be found in the book: *Learning Thai with Original Thai Words,* Chapter 13.

2.3.3 Action verbs

Action verbs are verbs that express actions like *to run, to work, to dance.*

2.3.4 State verbs

State verbs describe a state that usually lasts for some time. Some common examples where the state is described are: *to be (He is tall)*, *to have (I have fever)*, *to feel (I feel good)*. See Chapter 13.

2.3.5 Compound verbs

Compound verbs are used frequently in Thai in the sense that two verbs together form a new meaning. **dâai** ได้ is commonly used as compound verb with many other verbs. When using the compound verb in Thai, the structure is quite tight. This means that we usually cannot put other words between the two verbs.

2.4 Adjectives

2.4.1 Adjectives as adjectives

Adjectives in Thai can be used as *adjectives* as we understand them in English. Adjectives usually answer the question "what kind?". Example: *good, beautiful, happy*. **dâai** ได้ can be placed directly before an adjective in order to make an adjective become an adverb. See Chapter 11.

2.4.2 Adjectives as verbs

Adjectives in Thai can be used as *verbs*. In Thai, an adjective can play the role of the English verb *to be*. For the sentence to be complete, all you need is a subject and an adjective. There is no need for any verb as such. A similar structure is not possible in English. See Chapter 13.

2.4.3 Adjectives as adverbs

Adjectives in Thai can be used as *adverbs*. In Thai adjectives can play the role of an adverb of manner. In Thai when an adjective follows an action verb, "good" becomes *well*, "beautiful" becomes *beautifully* and "slow" becomes *slowly*.

2.5 Adverbs

2.5.1 Adverbs of time

Adverbs of time tell us *when* the action happened, will happen or perhaps that it is happening now. Examples: *yesterday, two days ago, tomorrow, nowadays.* In this book we usually call *adverbs of time "time words".*

2.5.2 Adverbs of frequency

Adverbs of frequency are used to tell us *how often* the action happens. Examples: *often, regularly, always.* In this book we usually call *adverbs of frequency "time words of frequency".*

2.5.3 Adverbs of place

Adverbs of place are used to tell us *where* the action happens. Examples: *far, near.*

2.5.4 Adverbs of manner

Adverbs of manner are used to tell us *how and in what way* the action happens. Examples: *slowly, well, gently.* See Chapter 12.

2.6 Prepositions

Both Thai and English use *prepositions* like *in, to, above, for.* See Chapter 15.

2.7 Conjunctions

Conjunction words such as *and, or, but, until* are used to connect two sentences. See Chapters 16 and 20.

3 Making sentences

In oder to make correct sentences, there are a few basic English terms which may prove helpful to know while learning Thai.

3.1 Simple subject

The *simple subject* is a *noun* or a *pronoun*. It is a person or thing that actively performs the action, the one who is in charge.

3.2 Simple predicate

The *simple predicate* is a *verb*, which describes or tells something about the subject. In Thai an adjective can be both a predicate and an adjective at the same time. No separate verb, as we understand it in English, is needed.

3.3 Object

3.3.1 Direct object

The term *direct object* is used for something which is given.

3.3.2 Indirect object

The term *indirect object* is used for the person to whom the direct object is given.

3.4 Subject-verb-object in the sentence

As you will learn in this book, the subject or the object can be dropped in Thai if understood from the context.

3.5 Tenses in English

The term *tense* in English is used to describe tenses such as *past, present* and *future*. The semantic meaning of the word *tense* is that the verb changes form when different tenses are used in English.

3.6 Tenses in Thai

The grammar rules in Thai are very straightforward. For instance, the verbs are not conjugated, there are no tenses for verbs, there are no plural forms for nouns and no genders or articles like *a, an* or *the*.

In Thai the *tense* (past, present, future) is made clear by *words*. We conveniently use the English word *tense* when referring to time in

Thai. We may say this is a past tense, even though there are no tenses in Thai as such. So, please do not get stuck with the definition of the English word *tense*. After all we are taking about the past, present or future. See Chapter 17.

3.7 Context

Context can be *verbal* or *social* or both. We use the word *context* in this book in a sense that the speaker takes into account the surroundings in which the conversation takes place and adapts her or his language to suit that context. Therefore, much maybe already understood and not everything needs to be spoken out.

3.8 Short form

We use the *short form* in the sense that when the context is clear, some words, which can be understood from the context, are dropped or left out.

3.9 Idiomatic expressions

Idiomatic expressions are informal ways to convey meanings. An idiomatic phrase may have a different meaning than the words in it. Idiomatic expressions give some juice to the expression.

3.10 Gerund

Gerund is a grammatical term used in English for nouns that are formed from verbs by the ending *-ing* such as *giving*. This kind of noun (gerund) can be a subject or an object in a sentence. In Thai, we form nouns from verbs by placing the prefix **kaan** การ before the verb. **kaan dâai** การได้ is translated into English as *getting*.

3.11 Genitive/possessive case

The term *genitive* is used to show *possession*. In English it is usually formed by adding *'s* after a noun or by placing the word *of* before the noun. In Thai the possessive form is created by the word **kɔ̌ɔng** ของ *of*.

3.12 Polite particles

In Thai *polite particles* are used frequently. The most common are **khâ** ค่ะ and **khráp** ครับ. They are not very easy to translate into English. Therefore, we have not given an exact English translation for them in our "word for word" translations. The overall meaning is close to the English word *please*. The polite particles in Thai are used grammatically a different way to the English word *please*. Their usage and "semantic boundaries" are much wider.

4 Other terms

4.1 Schwa

Even though the *schwa* is the most common vowel sound in English, this term is not usually known by native speakers of English language since phonetics is not commonly taught in schools while spelling is. The schwa is a short neutral vowel sound used in English. The sound depends on the consonant it is attached to. A good example is the letter "a" in the word *about*. However, the same letter is pronounced very differently in words such as *can, sad, make, article* where it is not the schwa. The vowel sounds are very clear and distinct in Thai and they cannot be blurred or changed to anything else like schwa in English.

If you are interested in phonetics and how to make correct Thai sounds, you may like to read the book:

22 Secrets of Learning Thai – Complete Guide to Sounds, Tones and Thai Writing System

◊

Bibliography

Becker, Benjawan Poomsan. Thai for Beginners.
Paiboon Publishing, California, 1995.

Becker, Benjawan Poomsan. Thai for Intermediate
Learners. Paiboon Publishing, California, 1998.

Becker, Benjawan Poomsan. Thai for Advanced
Learners. Paiboon Publishing, California, 2000.

Burusphat Somsonge. Reading and Writing Thai.
Institute of Language and Culture for Rural Development,
Mahidol University, Bangkok, 2006.

Dhyan, Manik. 22 Secrets of Learning Thai – Complete Guide to
Sounds, Tones and Thai Writing System, Dolphin Books, 2014.

Dhyan, Manik. Learning Thai with hâi ให้. Dolphin Books, 2016.

Dhyan, Manik. Learning Thai with dâai ได้ Book I.
Dolphin Books, 2017.

Dhyan, Manik. Learning Thai with dâai ได้ Book II.
Dolphin Books, 2018.

Higbie, James & Thinsan Snea. Thai Reference Grammar:
The Structure of Spoken Thai. Orchid Press, Bangkok, 2003.

James, Helen. Thai Reference Grammar.
D.K. Editions & Suk's Editions, Bangkok, 2001.

Kanchanawan, Nitaya & Eynon, Matthew J. Learning Thai A Unique
and Practical Approach. Odeon Store, Bangkok, 2005.

Ponmanee, Sriwilai. Speaking Thai for Advanced Learner. Thai
Studies Center, Chiang Mai Universtity, Chiang Mai, 2001.

Smyth, David. Thai: An Essential Grammar.
Routledge, London and New York, 2002.

Smyth, David. Teach Yourself Thai.
Hodder Headline, London, 2003.

22 Secrets of Learning Thai

– Complete Guide to Sounds, Tones and Thai Writing System

Twenty-two Secrets of Learning Thai teaches you all the sounds used in spoken and written Thai. It includes 20 consonant sounds, 18 pure vowel sounds, all special vowels and vowel combinations. It points out the main obstacles for learners, for example which Thai sounds are most difficult for an English speaker to produce. It then gives you handy tips to help overcome these difficulties. Much care has been taken to describe each sound in phonetic as well as in practical terms so that everyone should be able to grasp the correct way to produce Thai sounds.

The book has been designed so that it can be used by all levels of Thai learners. It contains a special exercise section, which teaches you in a step by step manner how to learn to read Thai script. At the same time all the Thai tone rules are taught in theory and practice. The student will get to know the most common Thai consonant symbols as well as rare symbols mostly borrowed from Indic languages, Pali and Sanskrit.

The book includes two audio CDs which feature more than 500 words spoken by native speakers to give you examples of how the words are produced in practice. In addition to individual words, the audio CDs feature many of the most common expressions used by Thai people in everyday conversation.

This book is suitable for self-study and can also be used as an aid in the classroom. It contains a vast number of tips to assist you in learning Thai and understanding some of the crucial cultural aspects of the language.

This book and CDs will set you on the road to confident Thai language learning.

22 Secrets of Learning Thai

– Learning Thai with hâi ให้

hâi ให้, along with words like dâai ได้, lέεu แล้ว and kɔ̂ɔ ก็, is one of the most important words in the Thai language.

When speaking Thai, it is important to understand the correct usage of the verb hâi ให้ in everyday speech.

One simple way to use the verb hâi ให้ is *to give something to someone*. It is used in a similar manner as the English verb *to give*.

In addition, hâi ให้ is used as a causative verb which has several different meanings depending on the situation, and the way it is spoken. It can be translated into English as *to let, to allow, to make* and even *to order* or *to force someone to do something*.

In some situations hâi ให้ is better translated into English as the preposition *for*, as in *for you, for me*, etc. It is also often used in idiomatic phrases where it carries no meaning itself but denotes only the sense of a command.

Thais use the verb hâi ให้ in an intuitive way in a variety of situations in order to express feelings, wishes, commands and nuances of meaning while communicating with each other every day.

If you learn this word well, you will be rewarded.

22 Secrets of Learning Thai

– Learning Thai with dâai ได้

Book I, Secrets 1–14

Whether you are a beginner or an advanced learner, you certainly want to learn to speak Thai fluently. This book will take you a long way towards your goal.

dâai ได้ is one of the most common words in Thai. It is a multifunctional helping verb and is used by Thais in several different ways. It has many distinct meanings depending on where it is placed in a sentence and which other words are used with it. With this book you won't just learn how to use dâai ได้ but will also acquire a deeper knowledge of the Thai language in general.

Included are:

- complete and informative written examples
- audio spoken by native speakers
- highlights and explanations of dâai's ได้ usage
- sections of simple and easy to understand advice
- useful hints and tips on dâai ได้ and the spoken Thai language

Furthermore, you will get to see the language "through the eyes of dâai ได้". Study this book and you will be rewarded; your Thai friends will be amazed at your deep understanding of the subtleties of their language.

22 Secrets of Learning Thai

– Learning Thai Tenses with dâai ได้

Book II, Secrets 15–22

Whether you are a beginner or an advanced learner, you will surely want to learn to speak Thai fluently. In order to do this, it is vital to use time words and tense markers correctly.

The English term *tense* is also a handy way to talk about past, present and future activities in Thai, even though there are no *tenses* as such in the Thai language. When compared to English, Thai tenses are expressed very differently.

It is often said that dâai ได้ denotes a past tense. However, it would be better not to think of dâai ได้ as the past tense marker since it can also be used to refer to present or future events.

To help you speak Thai fluently the Book II includes:

- complete and informative written examples
- audio spoken by native speakers
- highlights and explanations of dâai's ได้ usage
- sections of simple and easy to understand advice
- useful hints and tips on dâai ได้ and the spoken Thai language

Books I and II complement each other. However, each book has a different focus. In Book I, Secrets 1–14, we introduced dâai ได้ and explained where it should be placed in sentences. dâai ได้ has several grammatical functions; hence, it also has several meanings depending on the context. In Book II, Secrets 15–22, we focus on tenses.

Have fun while you study them both; then, you will understand how Thais express themselves in everyday life!

Learning Thai Quickly and Easily

with Original Thai Words

Do you want to learn to speak Thai as naturally as Thais do? Thai is not as difficult as you may think! If you follow the guidelines of this book, you will acquire a basic knowledge of the language in just a few weeks.

Students, usually, face several obstacles when studying Thai. In this book, we shall explain clearly what these obstacles are and how to overcome them. We shall also point out what you need to know and what you may ignore when learning to speak Thai. This will ensure your time and effort is focused on the things that really matter. You will be in a position to make an informed decision on how to proceed and deepen your language skills.

We use a simple and direct method which is easy to comprehend. You don't have to master the complex Thai writing system in order to speak Thai fluently. In this book, we concentrate on "original Thai words" which form a very important part of the Thai vocabulary and are used by Thais every day in conversation.

The book is designed in such a way that it can be used by both beginners and by those who have already reached intermediate level.

Included are:

- written examples and sentences
- audio spoken by native speakers
- highlights, explanations and examples on "how the language works"
- simple and easy to understand advice
- hints and tips on spoken Thai language
- "Take it further" section which includes many more tips on how to proceed with your studies

Now, you can tell all your friends that learning Thai can be easy. Read this book and you will discover how!

22 Secrets of Learning Thai books:

- Complete Guide to Sounds, Tones and
  Thai Writing System (2014)

- Learning Thai with hâi ให้ (2016)

- Learning Thai with dâai ได้ Book I
  Secrets 1–14 (2018)

- Learning Thai Tenses with dâai ได้ Book II
  Secrets 15–22 (2018)

- Learning Thai Tenses with lɛ́ɛu แล้ว (coming 2020)

- Learning Thai with kɔ̂ɔ ก็ (coming 2021)

Learning Thai Quickly and Easily:

- Learning Thai with Original Thai Words (2019)

- Learning Thai with English Words (coming 2020)

- Learning Thai with Foreign Words
  Pali, Sanskrit, Khmer, Chinese... (coming 2022)

For more information

Publisher:

www.dolphinbooks.org
info@dolphinbooks.org

www.thaibooks.net
www.facebook.com/22Secrets